the James River in Richmond

By John Bryan

Charles Creek Publishing 2023

Book Design by ThinkFast LLC

ISBN: 978-0-9987376-2-1

Library of Congress Control Number: 2022915696

First Printing: January 2023 / Printed in Canada

DISCLAIMER/WARNING: Much effort has been spent in making this book as accurate as possible. But there may still be mistakes — typographical as well as informational. This book should be used only as a general guide to enjoying the urban James River, and not as the ultimate source of advice or information. This book's purpose is to introduce the reader to Richmond's James River and to provide entertainment. The author and publisher shall not be liable or responsible for any damage or loss caused to any person or persons by the information contained in this book.

If you are not in agreement with this disclaimer, you may return this book to the publisher for a refund.

If you intend to go on or in the river, first determine the river level at Westham Gauge. (Google James River Westham Gauge.) If the level is above 5 feet, it is highly recommended that you wear a Coast Guard approved personal flotation device, and above 9 feet you shouldn't go on the river unless you're an expert. The river becomes more and more dangerous as it rises higher and higher above 5 feet.

Ryan Abrahamsen of Terrain360 partnered with Riverside Outfitters and Friends of James River Park to create a three-times-daily look at the urban river's water level, water temperature, air temperature, and weather forecast via a Twitter and Instagram feed entitled HowsTheJamesRVA.

If you encounter an "issue" in James River Park that warrants attention, call the James River Park System office (804) 646-6443 and/or submit a "Report an Issue" form that can be found on the website jamesriverpark.org. If immediate police attention is needed, call 911. If non-emergency police attention is needed, call (804) 646-5100.

This book is dedicated to **Angelina** ...

~~~~~~~~~~~~~~~~~~~~~~~

... and to **JC**, who continues to spice my enjoyment of the James River in Richmond.

This was the first time at the Skills Course on Belle Isle for twins Kit (on ramp) and Clay Johnson. Parents Dan and Lauren, both from Ohio, met after they moved to RVA more than a decade ago. Their courtship included outings in the James River Park System. As a family they also swim, hike, and "have fun on the rocks."

Most importantly, this book is dedicated to all of the children pictured herein:

Aiden	Ethan	Josiah	Luke
Asher	Ezekial	Josie	Milo
Ashley	F	Jude	Mira
Beau	Felicity	Julian	Nolan
Benlen	Fiore	Kaysen	Olivia
Caroline	Gabriel	Kendall	Owen
Carson	Gavin	Kennedy	Parker
Carter	George	Kieran	Ryan
Cash	Graham	Kit	Sean
Cillian	Hank	L	Skylar
Clay	Harry	Leighton	Stella
Dani	Henry	Lelle	Tobias
Eddie	Isaiah	Levin	Tonia
Eleanor	James	Lilian	Trinity
Eli	Jamari	Lincoln	Wilder
Emma	Jayden	Lola	

May their lives be filled with enjoyment of the river and an ongoing stewardship of its natural wonders.

Richmonders (left to right) Jamari, Juju, Josiah and Vince, pictured here on the Tyler Potterfield Memorial Bridge, also enjoy cycling, hiking, swimming, and kayaking.

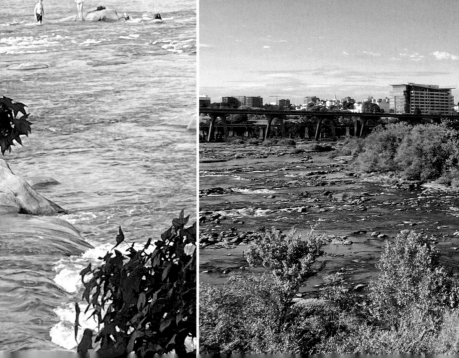

Special Thanks

Major funding from the E. Rhodes and Leona B. Carpenter Foundation helped launch this book project and meet its goal to provide 5,000 free copies to 16 nonprofit organizations that requested books to support their missions. Appreciation goes to the James River Association for providing its fiscal agency for the Carpenter Foundation funding. Additional generous funding from Brooks Smith and Jayne and Bobby Ukrop has enabled 1,000 additional free books to be given to RVA's Spanish-language communities. And an important grant from the Dominion Energy Charitable Foundation to Friends of James River Park is funding hundreds of books for the Friends' programs.

I greatly appreciate those who provided various degrees of information, advice, assistance, etc. while I was putting this book together. They include (in alpha order) Erin Bagnell, Jack Berry, Scott Blackwell, Alex Dahm, Scott Dickens, Elvira De la Cruz, Bill Draper, Scott Firestine, Chris Frelke, Giles Garrison, Patrick Griffin, Ralph Hambrick, Chris Hull, Jen Jimenez, Andrew Knight, Kyle McCann, Alex McCrickard, Dalila Medrano, Mike Ostrander, Tricia Pearsall, Matt Perry, Shep Roeper, Matt Rosenberg, Josh Stutz, Kevin Tobin, Greg Velzy, Charles Ware, Sally Wetzler, Ralph White, Bryce Wilk, Richard Woods, as well as many of the persons who allowed me to photograph them for the book.

I am grateful to those who provided content for special writings in the book: Rob Carter, Alex Dahm, Scott Dickens, Bill Draper, Chris Frelke, Giles Garrison, Patrick Griffin, Ralph Hambrick, Chris Hull, Tim Kaine, Isabel Levengood, Jon Lugbill, Alex McCrickard, Jamie McGrath, Fred Orelove, Tricia Pearsall, Shep Roeper, Bill Street, Greg Velzy, Sally Wetzler, and Ralph White.

Thanks to all of the folks whose photos are included in this book. Mostly strangers to me at the time,

Stuart and Pamela Davis, natives of New York and Maine, and now residents of Arlington, travel to the shores of Richmond's James River every year for the Richmond Folk Festival: "How wonderful to have something like this in the heart of the city!"

David B. Robinson

they said yes to my requests for their photos and information.

Thanks also to David B. Robinson, CPA, who not only does my taxes, but has also been a valuable partner for several of my philanthropic projects — including this guidebook. David has my appreciation for his ongoing consultation, especially for his suggestion that this book should have a Spanish language section. (Additional thanks to Arissa Lopez and Ana Ines King for Spanish language consultation!) David has also given personal energies and resources that are saving thousands of dollars in the costs associated with this book's distribution.

One of David's loves is RVA, especially its history, and for ten years (2009-2019) when he was not CPA-ing, he captained the *Martha Washington* for Venture Richmond's Riverfront Canal Cruises along the Kanawha Canal in Downtown Richmond, and was featured in an eight-minute segment on "CBS Sunday Morning" on January 15, 2018. David has my appreciation for helping with this book and for the many ways he contributes to the vitality of RVA. (www.greatcpa.com)

I salute the 16 nonprofit organizations that are putting their 5,000 books to good use in support of their missions. Beyond Boundaries, for example, is using the books in their work providing urban James River adventures such as float trips, for persons with developmental disabilities, at-risk youth, persons in recovery programs, etc. The Science Museum of Virginia is using the books in its educational programs. And the Richmond Public Library is providing books, free by request, to libraries of all types throughout the Richmond region. The other nonprofit organizations that are using the book are: Autism Society of Central Virginia, Blue Sky Fund, Friends of James River Park, Friends of Pump House, James River Association, James River Outdoor Coalition, James River Park System, Richmond Cycling Corps, rvaMORE, Sierra Club Virginia Chapter, Sportable, Virginia Capital Trail Foundation, and Virginia Department of Wildlife Resources.

And finally, the engaging visible appearance of this book, inside and out, is the work of designer Will Arnold, whose smiling professionalism, remarkable work ethic, and sincere enthusiasm have been invaluable to this project. ≈

Apology from the Author

I apologize for not being able to include in this book lots of worthy stuff AND for mistakes and omissions that I will no doubt discover later. I welcome your corrections and suggestions. Please send them to me at jbryanfish@aol.com.

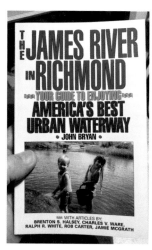

In 1997 when I published my 326-page book, *THE JAMES RIVER IN RICHMOND — YOUR GUIDE TO ENJOYING AMERICA'S BEST URBAN WATERWAY,* our urban river and its surroundings were far less popular and "developed" than they are today. The North Bank Trail didn't exist then. Neither did the 14th Street Takeout, the Universal Access Ramp at Huguenot Flatwater, the Slave Trail, the Canal Walk, Belle Isle's Skills Area, the T. Tyler Potterfield Memorial Bridge, and on and on. And Internet content was in its infancy. Back then there was far less information to include in a guidebook.

This year the James River Park System will receive more than two million visits. The events alongside the river — Richmond Folk Festival,

▼PICTURED BELOW: Ruth Savino (left), and Donna Feller on a hill overlooking the river at their volunteer posts at the Richmond Folk Festival. Their thoughts about this volunteer gig? "Oh my lord, it's the happiest time!" grinned Ruth.

Dominion Energy Riverrock, Que Pasa Festival, and on and on — will have more than a million attendees. Our urban river has become a <u>national</u> destination for cyclists, paddlers, climbers, historians, etc. and a <u>local</u> destination for every slice of life. And *Outside Magazine* has named Richmond as "America's most progressive, adventurous, and livable river town."

All of which means that today there are a zillion things worthy of inclusion in a James River guidebook — certainly enough material for at least ten volumes. But due to the constraints of only one volume, I had to omit a great deal of important material. I hereby apologize for this guidebook's inability to include a lot of worthy material, much of it from the following categories.

River Heroes — While developing this book, I continually heard the following: "Your book just HAS to include information about all the things that (name) did to make our urban river wonderful." "You MUST interview (name) as part of your research." I can list hundreds of names of persons who fit these categories. And there are

Ralph White demonstrating Turtle Talk in 1993.

thousands of others whose work and dedication have had key roles in the vitality of Richmond's James River. Some of these persons even have Elvis and Cher-level names — persons such as Ralph, Brent, Patti, Sue, R.B., Newton, and many more. You can read about many of these persons in wonderful previously-published books. (See this book's section on BOOKS.) I've chosen to refer you to those books to read about the good persons to whom we owe gratitude, and to focus THIS book's content simply on enjoying the river.

History — Today there is a robust presence of tasteful signage along the river that documents a great many aspects of our urban river's history: its artifacts and structures, its persons and events, and its roles in industry and recreation. This guidebook presents only a basic overview of the river's history as well as a few deeper dives. Google can point you to much more information on the river's historical smorgasbord.

Maps — Various websites contain all sorts of maps of the urban James and its surroundings: trail maps, climbing maps, cycling maps, parking maps, paddling maps, etc. The fact is that a detailed ALL-purpose map not only doesn't exist, but probably isn't possible. And even for the great printed maps that do exist, there are continual enhancements and additions and modifications that make such maps quickly out of date. Google can find continually updated mapping information.

Politics — Here are some of the things folks have told me as I prepared this book. "You MUST write about the CSO (combined sewer overflow) situation and its progress and its future." "You're going to talk about the constant struggle regarding whether to keep the James River Park as natural and wild as possible or to make it as accessible

as possible, right?" "What are you going to say about a need for ordinances that prescribe exactly what permits are required in order to swim, float, or paddle during the various river levels?" And of course, "You have to address the James River Park's need for more funding from public sources." Sorry, but I've determined that, as important as political issues are, this book isn't where I'll address them.

Details, Details, Details — Although there are folks who can describe every rapid and rock and hazard from Huguenot Flatwater to 14th Street, and can do so for every water level, this book doesn't have room for such detail. And although I have a current list of the nearly

200 bird species that have been seen along the urban James, this book doesn't have room for the list. It doesn't contain Newton Ancarrow's list of the hundreds of species of wildflowers. It doesn't contain the in-depth description that's presented during tours of the Pump House. And it doesn't describe every twist and turn and over and under of the river's miles and miles of trails. My hope is that the book provides just enough information to get you started and simultaneously just enough to cause you to learn more on your own.

The Future — There is an extremely comprehensive Master Plan for the James River Park System and also a Richmond Riverfront Plan. There are hopes and dreams and strategic plans for all sorts of things related to our urban river: the Pump House, the Canal Walk, Mayo's Island, the canal from Tredegar to Maymont, commercial recreational use of the river, hydro power, and on and on and on. The only thing this guidebook will say about the future is that it's filled with promise — promise for an ever-more-healthy, ever-more-enjoyable, ever-more-appreciated, and ever-more-beneficial urban James River.

Really Important Stuff — My research has included stacks and stacks of written materials, lots of interviews, and seemingly endless personal experiences. But I am certain that there are things that I've overlooked or missed or forgotten about or simply didn't know about — really important things. As soon as this book goes to press, I'll no doubt start discovering them. They, and you, have my apology. ≈

Glossy Abelia can grow to 2 to 6 feet tall; it's resistant to deer and attracts butterflies.

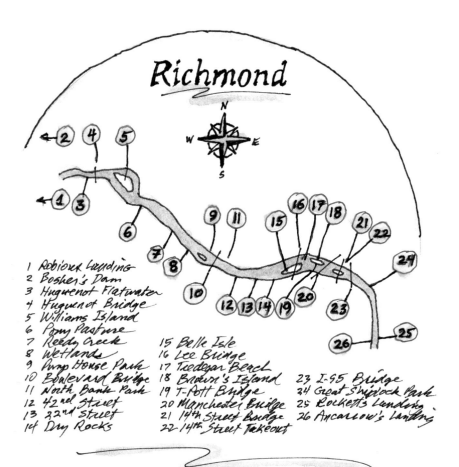

Richmond

1 Robious Landing
2 Bosher's Dam
3 Huguenot Flatwater
4 Huguenot Bridge
5 Williams Island
6 Pony Pasture
7 Reedy Creek
8 Wetlands
9 Pump House Park
10 Boulevard Bridge
11 North Bank Park
12 42nd Street
13 22nd Street
14 Dry Rocks
15 Belle Isle
16 Lee Bridge
17 Tredegar Beach
18 Brown's Island
19 T-Pott Bridge
20 Manchester Bridge
21 14th Street Bridge
22 14th Street Takeout
23 I-95 Bridge
24 Great Shiplock Park
25 Rockett's Landing
26 Ancarrow's Landing

Geographical Note

Although the James River stretches nearly 350 miles across Virginia, this guidebook pertains only to the 11-mile portion of the James River that has both shorelines within Richmond's city limits — roughly from the Huguenot Bridge to Rocketts Landing. The city limits on the south/west side of the river stretch an additional few miles both upstream and downstream, but there is limited public access on that side of the river. The book does include one area that is not in Richmond's city limits: Robious Landing Park which is 12 miles upstream from Bosher's Dam.

In the COMPANIES AND ORGANIZATIONS section of this book you'll find many websites that have a variety of excellent maps, both micro and macro, ranging from mountain bike maps of specific trails to paddling maps of the river's routes to climbing maps for the Manchester Wall. Richmond's James River is so diverse and so filled with all sorts of opportunities that a single all-purpose map isn't possible. And of course Website maps (that can be continually modified) have a huge advantage over printed maps.

This guidebook's only map is one that I've hand-drawn here. It provides a quick look at the approximate locations of some of the most popular areas along the James River in Richmond. ≈

Foreword
BY JON LUGBILL

(The American Canoe Association says that Jon Lugbill, Executive Director of Sports Backers, "is generally recognized as the best paddler to ever compete in whitewater canoeing." And he's the only paddler to ever be pictured on a box of Wheaties!)

Recently I paddled on the James River just as the sun was rising on an already balmy August weekday. Morning mist lingered just above the flatwater and the only sound I was conscious of was my paddle slicing through the flatwater. Suddenly, my meditative state was happily interrupted by a prehistoric-looking 7-foot sturgeon that fully breached through the mist with the city's skyline as its backdrop. And then, in a split second, nature's masterpiece took a comedic turn with a massive belly-flop before submerging. On another summer outing just after sunrise, I was ferrying across the river in a particularly rocky area. I often saw geese and ducks feeding around the rocks, but that day, as I glided across on a wave to an eddy behind a large rock, I was met with fur, not feathers. A sleek otter was enjoying its breakfast when I unknowingly interrupted its meal. It side-eyed me as it slipped into the water and swam away. A few seconds later, I heard it chirping a warning to its otter friends of my presence. I marvel that these experiences can happen within a couple of miles of my house in the City of Richmond.

I guess it is not surprising there is so much wildlife in the James River these days. Gone are the decades of abuse from pollution, and the river has had a chance to cleanse itself. It is not uncommon to have 25 feet of visibility in the river. People snorkel below Pipeline Rapids to check out the fish and crabs. The irony is that these wonders of nature are located in the center of downtown Richmond with 20-storey office and apartment buildings on the river banks.

On another river excursion, I was paddling in a dragon boat (a 40-foot-long canoe) with 15 other people on the flatwater section right by the apartments at Rocketts Landing. An osprey entertained us by performing a high dive into the water and emerging with a freshly caught fish. Just as we were congratulating the osprey, a bald eagle torpedoed out of a nearby tree and attacked the osprey in mid-air. During the air battle, the osprey dropped the fish, and the eagle tucked its wings to dive through the air like a missile before extending its talons to grab the fish off the water. We couldn't believe it! This time, we congratulated ourselves for being in the right place at the right time to witness the drama. Now, that's a good enough story, but there's more, and it's good that there are 15 witnesses to back it up. After the eagle reaped its fish reward, a red-tailed hawk flew onto the scene and attacked the bald eagle. The hawk stole the

fish right from the talons of the exhausted eagle. The dejected eagle flew away, and the hawk soared over to a tree to enjoy its spoils. It's as if we were living in the middle of a wildlife video with David Attenborough narrating the whole thing.

One of the things I love about the James River in downtown Richmond is the dichotomy between the beauty and solitude of nature and the ability for thousands of people to celebrate the river at the same time. In 2009, Sports Backers created the Dominion Energy Riverrock outdoor sports and music festival to highlight the outdoor recreation amenities in and along the James River. This event showcases Richmond's unique urban park and wildlife oasis in the heart of downtown. The event has taken off and regularly attracts 100,000 people to Richmond's riverfront over the course of three days. Encouraging Richmond area residents to celebrate the James River is a very easy task. Ask anyone around here and you will hear pride in their voices about their wild adventures in the James River Park.

I often warn out-of-town visitors that the James River Park is wild. By that, I mean not just that the downtown park is full of wildlife, but also that it holds many adventure opportunities. It's fun to hike around Belle Isle and rock hop on the rugged, barren dry riverbed south of the island. And the North Bank and Buttermilk trails are rated as expert mountain biking experiences. The Manchester Wall

climbing area provides an ideal urban setting to learn outdoor climbing skills. And, of course the rapids in downtown provide an unexpected challenge with difficulty being from Class III to Class V, depending on the water level. It's easy to forget you're in the middle of the city, but at the end of a ride or hike, it's nice to remember that a coffee shop, brewery, or restaurant is close by!

James River Park provides an oasis for me to get my outdoor adventure sports fix almost daily. For me it doesn't matter if I'm paddling the rapids of the lower James, trail running or mountain biking on the challenging single track or going for a walk with my dog, the James River never fails to provide respite from the busy life of a region of 1.3 million people. No wonder that *Outside Magazine* named Richmond, Virginia the nation's Best Outdoor River Town!

Recently my wife Gillian and I went to have a meal at the Lilly Pad at Kingsland Marina. While we enjoyed our lunch, we watched sturgeon leaping out of the water and splashing back into the river. It struck me that this was our first time eating here. Once again, we were doing something on the James River for the first time. This outing has inspired us to double down on discovering all that the James River has to offer. ≈

Introduction
BY TIM KAINE

(Richmonder Tim Kaine has served as U.S. Senator from Virginia since 2013. He has been a Richmond City Council member, Richmond Mayor, Virginia Lieutenant Governor, and Virginia Governor, and was the Democratic candidate for U.S. Vice President in 2016.)

John Bryan's 1997 edition of this book sits on a coffee table in my living room where the sound of rushing water from the James River is a constant companion. The cover is torn and its pages are creased from 25 years of use. I still rely on it to plan adventures on the James in and near Richmond. When I heard of this 2023 edition, with the promise of new stories and history and excursions, I was filled with a sense of pleasant anticipation.

Photo provided by Tim Kaine

I moved from Kansas City to Richmond in 1984 to marry my wife Anne. I made a strong effort to convince her to come to Kansas City, the friendly and beautiful Midwestern city where my family still lives. But Anne had a secret weapon in this competition, the James River.

She knew how I reveled in the canoe trips of my youth, driving 4 hours to the Ozark Mountains to camp and fish along the Current, Jacks Fork and Buffalo Rivers. So she took me to Texas Beach for a picnic when I first visited in the summer of 1982. We watched swimmers and fishers, blue herons and boaters, enjoying the James. It was wilderness right in the heart of the city. And as we drove around town, I noticed an unusual proliferation of canoes and kayaks on car rooftops. I was hooked.

As we dated in the years before we married, we returned to the James many times—in Richmond, Scottsville,

Lynchburg. And we went to other rivers — the Maury, North Anna, South Anna, Appomattox, Tye. I could not believe how rich Virginia was in rivers — each with its own natural beauty and each with its own complicated and challenging history.

So we chose Richmond and I explained that it was due to finding the best combination of jobs here. But I knew then that the pull of the James was a powerful factor.

In nearly 40 years together, Anne and I have subconsciously centered our life around the James. Her folks gave us a red Old Town canoe for Christmas the first year of our marriage and it bears decades of nicks and scrapes from frequent runs from Pony Pasture to Reedy Creek.   We hike and birdwatch in James River Park. We bike along the Virginia Capital Trail. We've watched our three children learn to canoe, kayak and rock climb on Belle Isle, first as campers and later as counselors. We've held birthday parties and scavenger hunts on the banks. We've attended riverside concerts on Brown's Island and seen fireworks displays reflected in the tidal water near Rocketts Landing. We never tire of the James because it is different in every season and at every water level. And so are we.

During our years in Richmond, we've experienced an amazing renaissance of a proud river, long tarnished by pollution and neglect, reclaiming its status as Richmond's front porch, the very reason for its existence. The Clean Water Act, passed by Congress in October 1972 over a Presidential veto, laid the groundwork for vast improvement thereby demonstrating that environmental regulation and economic development need not conflict. So many James River stewards—people and organizations—have worked diligently to clean up the river, establish open space and parks, reclaim our historic canal system, construct hiking and biking trails, build up flood walls to protect vulnerable neighborhoods, breach old dams to allow fish to return to their ancient upstream homes, create historical signage and displays. As a city council member and Mayor, then Lieutenant Governor and Governor, and now Senator, I've been proud to play a role in many of these improvements. When I left the Governor's office in 2010, I made

sure that my official portrait shows me standing next to the river.

Now, the James River is recognized globally for its rebound. It won the prestigious Thiess International Riverprize award in 2019 as a tribute to both its history and its restoration. The bald eagle population along the James was once among the densest in North America but had virtually disappeared by the mid-1960's. Today it is healthy again and sightings of our national bird—together with hawks, falcons, ospreys, cormorants, herons, buzzards, ducks, geese and all manner of songbirds are daily, indeed hourly, occurrences in Richmond. The Atlantic sturgeon, thought to be extinct in the James and its tributaries just a few years ago, has made a remarkable comeback and September brings astounding displays as these massive prehistoric fish leap high out of the water below the Fall Line.

I canoed the entire 350 miles of the James in 2021—from Iron Gate in the Allegheny Mountains to Fort Monroe in the Chesapeake Bay—and witnessed the return of eagles and sturgeon and so much more.

The most important return, however, is by people seeking everyday fun and rejuvenation. Once we decided to reclaim the James and clean it up, it became the center of our city's identity, an object of joy and pride marked by the Richmond city flag's rendering of an heroic James River bateau captain. Now most Richmond families, like ours, accumulate wonderful lifetime memories from their moments along our beautiful waterway.

This new edition of John Bryan's classic river guide will make sure that popular embrace of the James continues. And we need it to continue.   The James still needs stewards. In recent years, the National Trust for Historic Preservation has listed 2 sites along the James on its annual list of America's most endangered historic places. The Monacan historic village Rassawek, at the confluence of the James and Rivanna Rivers in Fluvanna County, was almost converted into a water treatment facility a few years ago. Jamestown Island is threatened by sea level rise. Powerful advocacy by the Monacan Nation and their supporters averted the first threat and vigorous public policy to battle climate change will be needed to avert the second.

In the City of Richmond, the fight goes on to continue improving water quality by eliminating combined sewer overflows pouring into the James during extreme rain events, which are becoming more frequent here and elsewhere. Recent federal legislation has helped fund this decades-long effort but we can't yet claim victory.

The battles to save and improve the James are not over. Each generation of Richmonders will confront new challenges on the river and dig into their effort and creativity and pocketbooks to surmount them.

This updated guide to our river will sit on desks and bookshelves and coffee tables, frequently opened to inspire day trips and lifetime adventures. I confidently predict that many who undertake them will become as hooked on the James River as I became 40 years ago. And the pull of the river on those who enjoy its many virtues will guarantee that the James will continue to have stewards passionate about its protection. ≈

Amy and Tom Paquette and their children Henry (4, red shirt), James (3, blue), and Josie (10 months) live in Charlottesville, but love coming to RVA for family outings on Belle Isle. Henry and James enjoy taking their scooters on the mountain bike course. Amy (artist/educator/birder) and Tom (solar energy industry) smile as they reveal that their first "big dating adventure" was on Belle Isle. Amy's paintings can be found at www.amyshawleypaquette.com

Preface
BY JOHN BRYAN

(I wrote the following in 1996 for my first guidebook for the river. My thought is that it is still relevant.)

several years ago my friend Wimberly Brown, Professor Emeritus of History for the University of Georgia, told me that he had accepted an invitation to present a 20-minute lecture for the garden club of a rural South Georgia town. He smiled and shook his head as he told me they had selected a topic that, for him, was going to be difficult. They had asked him to speak for 20 minutes on the topic, "France."

Likewise, it is impossible to shoehorn the urban James River into a manageable book. But, even though this book has bitten off much more than it can chew, it has, nevertheless, bitten it off.

A hundred years ago the importance of our urban river was almost totally commercial. It provided a seaport, a power source, a raw materials source, and a waste site.

Today its importance is almost totally recreational. Our priority now is to preserve its beauty, its flora and fauna, its artifacts, its water quality, and its ambience. Things that didn't matter back then are now of priority importance to Richmond's leaders and citizens. The river is our most important amenity.

Why? It is of course because of the things discussed in this book: paddling and floating, hiking and biking, fishing and climbing, access and inclusion, history and nature, events and organizations, and on and on. But it is also for a much broader reason. All of those things,

plus the river's visual beauty, make Richmond a great place to live. And as the river helps attract new citizens and businesses, virtually everyone prospers.

RVA's James is the nation's best urban river. How do you confirm something like that? One way is to take my URBAN RIVER CHALLENGE later in this book. (Of course *Outside Magazine* confirmed it 16 years after I wrote this, naming Richmond #1 among the 50 river cities they considered.)

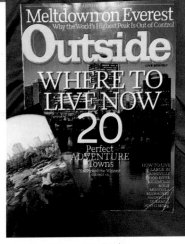

As a Richmonder I have three big responsibilities regarding the river. First I need to continue to learn more about it (so, for example, when an out-of-towner considers moving to Richmond I can talk with enthusiastic detail about the river). Second I need to make opportunities to tell other Richmonders about the river (so, for example, my neighbor will have already heard my safety recommendations about the river prior to innocently setting afloat). And third, I must step forward and be counted as I see opportunities for advocacy and preservation (as R.B. Young and friends did years ago when an expressway was in store for the river's shoreline).

▼PICTURED BELOW: **Kristen Beasley and daughters Kennedy (5) and Lelle (7) enjoying the river.**

May 24 is the anniversary of Christopher Newport's "discovery" of the falls of the James with his arrival at what is now urban Richmond. He and his crew viewed a clean river that was rich with vegetation and was a natural magnet to fish and wildlife and birds and of course the Algonquian Indians. There was no mechanized industry, no ocean trade, and no dumping. Today our river has come full circle and its health probably more closely resembles its discovery day than ever before.

If you haven't yet done so, select at least one aspect of our river and embrace it — first to enhance your own quality of life, and second for that of others. ≈

Andrew Knight with a James River smallmouth bass

JC Gilmore-Bryan along the river's sidewaters.

Passages Adventure Camper focused on the last drop of the Pipeline Rapids. Photo by Stephanie Garr-Adams

An Invitation to Families

Chris Frelke, Director of the City of Richmond's Department of Parks, Recreation and Community Facilities, offers the following encouragement for families: I invite you and your family to take a break from computers and tablets and reconnect with the outdoors along our James River in Richmond. Explore the rocks along the river, learn and talk about the history of the Slave Trail, take a trip on the river with an outfitter, and offer your children opportunities to embrace the majestic river's activities: hiking, biking, climbing, floating, paddling, history, nature, fishing, swimming, etc. Enjoying the James River in Richmond is transformative! ≈

Table of Contents

ACTIVITIES & INTERESTS

ANNUAL EVENTS

MUCH MORE

SECCIÓN DE LENGUA ESPAÑOLA

BONUS STORIES

CLOSING

Vintage Trevor Piersol

Places

In this section you'll find information about the well-known named places along the urban James: Pony Pasture, Texas Beach, T-Pott, etc. You can get a general idea of their locations by looking at my little hand-drawn map in the front pages of this book. And you'll find details about parking in this book's PARKING section. I encourage you to explore and discover additional "places": some that have been informally named (Poop Loop, for example), some that have obscure locations (Lost Garden, for example), and some that are well-used but unnamed (that huge area on the southwest side of the river beneath the I-95 Bridge, for example). And during your explorations I hope you'll find your own private "secret" place — a place that appears to have been undiscovered by anyone else, a place that exposes a bit of the seemingly undisturbed wilderness in the midst of our city. (Read THE SECRET SPOT later in this book.)

PLACES

Ancarrow's Landing

HISTORIC SLAVE TRAIL

This spring wildflower is known as sleepydick, nap-at-noon and common star-of-Bethlehem.

Located on the southwest side of the river at the end of Brander Street, Ancarrow's Landing has a huge parking lot (200+ cars), a concrete ramp for launching all kinds of boats , a historic riverside granite docking wall along which anglers and picnickers relax, the trailhead for the Slave Trail that follows a forested path upstream, and the trailhead for the "Poop Loop" that's a popular biking trail that heads southeast and is named for its proximity to Richmond's wastewater treatment facility.

The site was named for Newton Ancarrow who was a passionate naturalist who documented more than 400 species of wildflowers along the Richmond portion of the James River. He was also a designer and builder of speedboats at his facility, Ancarrow's Marine, that was located here. A co-founder of Reclaim the James, Inc., Ancarrow worked and advocated tirelessly for pollution and sediment control and many other environmental issues related to the health of the James.

ANCARROW'S LANDING

Eagle Scout Project Built by Spalding Hall Troop 64

Although Ancarrow's Landing doesn't offer opportunities for wading or swimming, it is nevertheless a highly visited area for other types of recreation including hiking, biking, fishing, bird-watching, picnicking, and simply relaxing in the abundant shady areas. Plus, it features beautifully designed interpretive signage about the area's historic importance as well as its fish and other flora and fauna. An important heads-up: each year during the entire month of April Ancarrow's Landing is crowded with vehicles launching boats and anglers casting from the fishing wall. Each April this part of the river is thick with fish in the annual spawning run of shad, stripers, and white perch, and anglers are rarely disappointed. ≈

Lesser celandine, also called fig buttercup, flowers along the river in the spring.

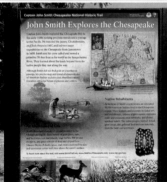

Fishing Tips from Chris Hull

✔ A one-inch, sixteenth-ounce, white curly-tail jig will catch every species on the upper James (upstream from 14th Street): sunfish, smallmouths, catfish, etc.

✔ A blue/chrome Rat-L-Trap is a great multi—species lure on the lower James (downstream from 14th Street).

✔ A yellow/brown/gold broken-back Rapala in all sizes is effective on all areas of the river.

VCU grads Amelia Gulding (sociology) and Emmie Curry (English) enjoy reading and sunbathing along the river. Belle Isle and Pony Pasture are two of their favorite areas.

HEADGATE CLEANE

Water leading to the power plant was kept clean by passing it through slats in the headgate called trash racks. Bits of wood can wear away the edges turbine blades and make them unbalanced. Repair w complicated and expensive.

This "mechanical rake" kept the trash racks clean of leaves and small debris. Notice how the steel teeth fit between the metal slats and could slide up and down. The wheels rode on the rails which now have handrails attached.

The log jam is now a home for fish, turtles, and

Sign funded by the students at Collegiate High

▲ PICTURED ABOVE, LEFT PHOTO: Three generations of Richmonders on Belle Isle: grandmother Gay Ford, an insurance arbitrator; son Frank Ford Jr. who enjoys many sections of the river; and grandson Ezekial Gilchrease (age 4, Frank's nephew).

Belle Isle

The 54-acre, family-friendly Belle Isle is accessed from the north side of the river by the footbridge beneath the Lee Bridge (parking lot on Tredegar Street, and additional street parking on 5th Street), and from the south side of the river by the bridge (pedestrian and emergency vehicles) located approximately ¼ mile along the path downstream from the parking lot at Riverside Drive and 22nd Street. Although Belle Isle is the most visited area of the James River Park System, its wooded trails and hideaways offer plenty of opportunities for solitude. Belle Isle offers trails for hiking and mountain biking, historical sites, fishing, rock climbing, picnicking, sunbathing, swimming, and an abundance of flora and fauna. Plus, its main loop, as well as a couple of concrete ramps to the water, are wheelchair accessible.

Belle Isle has many special features including a custom-built bicycle skills area; a quarry pond for fishing for bass, sunfish, and catfish; numerous historic sites and artifacts accompanied by interpretive signage; granite sunbathing rocks adjacent to the Class III Hollywood Rapids through which a seemingly continual succession of kayaks, rafts, paddleboards, and canoes traverse; a large, covered, multi-picnic-table area (immediately northwest of the Quarry Pond); swimming areas

including at First Break Rapids (just northwest of the Quarry Pond); and a multi-section granite climbing wall (on the south edge of the Quarry Pond).

Although getting to Belle Isle requires a good amount of walking or cycling, it's nevertheless continually populated with virtually every slice of life including families with very small children. Belle Isle is also very popular with dog owners.

When you visit Belle Isle, you may want to explore some of the narrow tributary trails, including up to the top of the island. You'll no doubt discover nooks and crannies that seem secret and untouched. ≈

PICTURED ABOVE AND BELOW: RVA natives Ashley Dunn and Emily Knabel have enjoyed the James River environs throughout their lives, including the Canal Walk and the Virginia Capital Trail. (Ashley has completed the full Trail!)

Projected Art

"Recontextualizing Richmond" is a collaborative public art initiative headed by Dustin Klein, pictured here, and partner Alex Criqui, "that brings together activists, artists, and historical institutions to elevate neglected historical narratives in Richmond, Virginia through works of light-based art" — as shown here during a multi-evening event on Belle Isle. Klein and Criqui gained national attention — including the cover of *National Geographic* magazine — by their artwork that projected an image of George Floyd onto Richmond's Robert E. Lee monument. More information about the organization can be found at reclaimingthemonument.com.

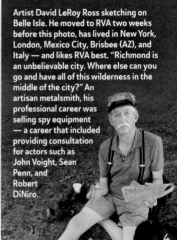

Artist David LeRoy Ross sketching on Belle Isle. He moved to RVA two weeks before this photo, has lived in New York, London, Mexico City, Brisbee (AZ), and Italy — and likes RVA best. "Richmond is an unbelievable city. Where else can you go and have all of this wilderness in the middle of the city?" An artisan metalsmith, his professional career was selling spy equipment — a career that included providing consultation for actors such as John Voight, Sean Penn, and Robert DiNiro.

4

Brown's Island

On the six-acre, grass-carpeted Brown's Island, located across the canal in downtown Richmond, you'll find hikers, bikers, picnickers, lunch-breakers, and all sorts of festivals, concerts, and other events. The Island is accessed by three bridges along Tredegar Street on the north side of the river: the canal headgate bridge just across the street from the American Civil War Museum, the 5th Street Footbridge where 5th Street meets Tredegar Street, and the Brenton S. Halsey Footbridge at the end of 7th Street. The Island can also be accessed from the south side of the river via the T. Tyler Potterfield Memorial Bridge (pedestrian and cycle).

Named for its first settler, Elijah Brown, who bought the land in 1826, the Island eventually became an industrial site with hydroelectric power and coal power facilities and also a paper mill. Hurricanes were a major factor in the Island's loss of industry, and in 1987 the Island became part of the James River Park System. The Island's first statuary artwork was "The Headman" by Richmond sculptor Paul DiPasquale. The most poignant public artwork on the Island today is the Emancipation and Freedom Monument, by Thomas Jay Warren, that highlights African American history and includes two compelling 12-foot bronze male and female figures that

represent newly-freed slaves.

One of the Island's best features is its southwestern access to the T. Tyler Potterfield Memorial Bridge — a footbridge that leads all the way across the river and provides stunning views of the river and its rapids, birds, and boaters. (See the T. Tyler Potterfield Memorial Bridge section of this book.)

A lot more information about Brown's Island can be found by searching "Brown's Island" at **www.venturerichmond.com**. ≈

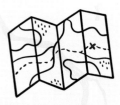

Host YOUR Event

Host an event or class or outing in James River Park? City permits are required to hold classes, conduct tours, or host any type of event in the James River Park and/or on the river.

Go to **rva.gov**, Parks & Recreation, Special Events.

▲ PICTURED ABOVE: Friends enjoying Friday Cheers on Brown's Island: Lilly Clem, former chef and now a student at UC Davis; Billy Rice, retired from media production with the State of Virginia and now a board member of JAMInc.; Reese Williams, host of "Shockoe Session Live;" drummers Scott Milstead and Ben Marcia; and Queon "Q" Martin, founder of Carter Magazine.

In recognition of Brenton S. Halsey, founding Chairman/CEO of James River Corporation and founding Chairman of the Richmond Riverfront Development Corporation. His vision, leadership and tenacity were the driving force behind the successful revitalization of the James River Riverfront and Richmond's Canal Walk.

This bridge has been made possible with the financial support of

MWV	McGuire Woods
Mary Morton Parsons Foundation	SunTrust Bank
The Cabell Foundation	Susan Williams
NewMarket	Venture Richmond
Dominion Resources	In addition to many other supporters.

Matt Scott, Senior Education Manager for the James River Association, and Lane Carasik, mechanical engineering faculty member at VCU, pictured here at the steps to Brown's Island, enjoy all of the urban river — especially Pony Pasture and especially tubing.

The Canal Walk

▼ PICTURED BELOW: Gabriel and sister Jacqueline Meeks and Davion Hutt enjoy the Canal Walk during Dominion Energy Riverrock. Gabriel, a reggae band member from Virginia Beach, enjoys mountain biking and hiking in the James River Park System. Jacqueline is a nursing student at Reynolds Community College. Davion, a former record-holder in track at William & Mary, sells AFLAC insurance and works at Richmond's Station 2 restaurant.

The Canal Walk, just over a mile long, parallels the Kanawha and Haxall Canals in downtown Richmond's business district and has multiple access points between 5th and 17th Streets — including wheelchair-accessible entrances at 5th, 10th, 12th, 14th and 16th Streets. The Walk is popular with bikers, joggers, walkers, tourists, history enthusiasts, and lunch-breakers. The Walk's attractions include public art, statues, interpretive signage and medallions about the area's history, restaurants, and canal cruises.

Prior to railroads, waterways were the major transportation trade routes westward, and canals were needed to bypass rocky rapids and falls. Richmond's canal system that bypassed the James River's seven miles of "falls" was the first towpath (tethered mules and horses walked the towpath while pulling the boats) canal system in the nation. Richmond's original canal system had wooden locks (later replaced), docks, and turning basins. All of this allowed boats to transport goods up- and downstream between Richmond and Lynchburg. Damage during the Civil War, along with the advent of railroads, spelled the end of the canal system as a reliable form of transportation.

The Canal Walk features 22 bronze medallions embedded along the path, each of which describes part of the area's history. For example, the "Belle Isle" medallion tells of the Civil War prisoners who were kept in Richmond — including as many as 8,000 in the camp on Belle Isle. The "Powhatan Chiefdom" medallion tells of the first residents of the area as early as 10,000 years ago. The "Confederate Laboratory" medallion reveals the hazards of loading gunpowder on Brown's Island and the explosion that killed 46 workers. And the "Haxall Millrace" medallion tells of the hydropower operation that ground wheat and made Richmond one of the world's largest flour exporters.

There is abundant public art along the Canal Walk including the Christopher Newport Cross that commemorates the May 24, 1607 landing of the ship of Christopher Newport and crew — the area's first Europeans. He planted a cross in honor of King James I in the vicinity of today's 14th Street Bridge. A uniquely interesting public artwork is in remembrance of, and tribute to, Henry "Box" Brown, a slave who mailed himself in a box north to freedom. And on the walls of a tunnel beneath an overhead bridge along the Canal Walk you'll see the abstract mural created by Marta Finkelstein. And there are additional murals including Hamilton Glass' "James, Is That You I Smell?" across from Casa del Barco restaurant.

Much more information about the Canal Walk can be found at **www.venturerichmond.com**. ≈

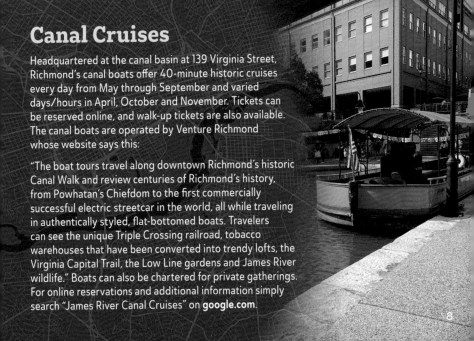

Canal Cruises

Headquartered at the canal basin at 139 Virginia Street, Richmond's canal boats offer 40-minute historic cruises every day from May through September and varied days/hours in April, October and November. Tickets can be reserved online, and walk-up tickets are also available. The canal boats are operated by Venture Richmond whose website says this:

"The boat tours travel along downtown Richmond's historic Canal Walk and review centuries of Richmond's history, from Powhatan's Chiefdom to the first commercially successful electric streetcar in the world, all while traveling in authentically styled, flat-bottomed boats. Travelers can see the unique Triple Crossing railroad, tobacco warehouses that have been converted into trendy lofts, the Virginia Capital Trail, the Low Line gardens and James River wildlife." Boats can also be chartered for private gatherings. For online reservations and additional information simply search "James River Canal Cruises" on **google.com**.

Dry Rocks

I love the Dry Rocks area. The river bordering the south side of Belle Isle is filled with a rock-hopper's fantasy of granite boulders — mostly dry when the river level is below five feet. The area's seemingly endless puddles, shallow pools, and pebble-carved holes in the boulders harbor all sorts of life, including catchable fish, as well as interesting river debris — some of it from far upstream and from distant years. No telling what you will find.

Years ago when I took my 10-year-old son and his friend on a scavenger hunt there, they found a very old recoilless rifle. My call to the police resulted in the arrival of the HazMat team and their big truck. Nothing exploded and nobody was injured.

The Dry Rocks area can be accessed from the 22nd Street parking lot (where 22nd meets Riverside) for James River Park, or better yet from the path where 21st Street meets Riverside

Vintage Thomas Bryan

PICTURED ABOVE, MIDDLE PHOTO: Richmonders Paul and L. (declined to give full names) enjoy Dry Rocks. Paul works at Grimké Seminary.

Drive. The walk down to the river includes a footbridge over the railroad tracks followed by a mostly paved or concreted path that goes both directions. Go to the right to get the best access to the Dry Rocks — beginning in 100 yards or so. This area is accessible to those who are nimble-footed. ≈

RC Rock Crawling

On a sunny Saturday at the Dry Rocks area of the river I encountered something I'd never seen along the river: RC Rock Crawling. Several men were remotely controlling little vehicles that were going up and down and over and around rocks and boulders. I learned that rock crawlers generally sell for hundreds of dollars, that there are amazing competitions, and that there are lots of videos on YouTube.

▲ PICTURED ABOVE: Richmonder Malcolm Turner, who grew up in Mosby Court and now lives in the West End, enjoys RC rock crawling in the Dry Rocks area.

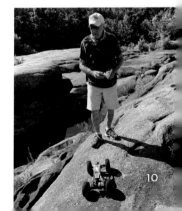

The Floodwall Walk

The Richmond Floodwall is constructed on both sides of the river, but the portion on the southwest side of the river, extending more than two miles, is the one that offers a top-of-the-wall and along-the-wall walkway with wonderful views of the river, great birdwatching and photography, easy walking and biking, and proximity to good fishing. Also you'll get great views of river activities such as kayaking, floating, and angling. And beneath the 14th Street Bridge and downstream during the month of April — the annual spawning run — you'll see the climb-down-the-rocks shoreline lined with anglers — and additional anglers in boats — catching shad and stripers. From the Floodwall you can see lots of small islands that provide wonderful habitat for migratory birds. You can also see Sharp's Island where the Sharp family's home was located for 75 years until being washed away by a flood. The island is now privately owned and is the only James River island in the city that provides legal camping via an Airbnb rental opportunity.

The Floodwall consists of both levee and actual wall. There are three primary ways to access it. One is downstream via the Slave Trail that travels from Ancarrow's Landing upstream to the I-95 Bridge and then onto the Floodwall. A second access

◀ PICTURED LEFT: Tourists beneath the Manchester Bridge at the end of the Floodwall: Richmonder Bryan Hill (tallest), a federal railroad inspector, and his Tennessee relatives (children, left to right) Eleanor, Carter, Isaiah, and Gabriel Hill; and adults (l-r) Lauren, Matthew, and Laurie Hill; and Chris Matthews.

is from Hull Street on the south side of the 14th Street Bridge at the small Floodwall Park that has a 15-car parking lot. There is also street parking available in the neighborhood — although it's likely that you'll need to search and then walk a ways. Just on the other side of the canal from the parking lot is a staircase that leads up to a nice overlook. From the Hull Street sidewalk there is a path that leads down toward the river and also under the bridge and onto the Floodwall pathway that goes downstream. To go upstream atop the Floodwall, you need to take the path adjacent to the western edge of the parking lot. In 100 yards or so you'll get to a stairway that leads to the top of the Floodwall and you can walk from there all the way upstream to the Manchester Bridge and continued trails including to the T. Tyler Potterfield Memorial Bridge. A third way to access the Floodwall is from the 20-car parking lot at 7th and Semmes. This lot is accessible from only one direction and is relatively obscure, and thus it often has vacancies. From the lot it's a fairly long but totally barrier-free distance to the Floodwall: more than 200 yards to a footbridge that crosses the railroad tracks, then once across the bridge another 200+ yards downhill to beneath the Manchester Bridge, and then another 50 or so yards to the actual Floodwall.

The Floodwall's entire length offers stunning panoramic views of the river and the city. More information can be found by searching Richmond Floodwall or Manchester Floodwall at **explanders.com**. ≈

Legend Brewing Co. (legendbrewing.com)

Legend Brewing Co., located at 321 W. 7th Street, is the oldest operating craft brewery in Virginia. Perched above the south shore of the downtown James, not far from the Manchester climbing wall and the T. Tyler Potterfield Memorial Bridge, its popularity among persons who enjoy the James River Park System is evidenced by its customers' cars that carry kayaks and bicycles, and by its groups of "regulars" that include climbers, fly-fishers, paddlers, cyclists, etc. In 2022 it premiered its "Raging James Pilsner" that provides funding for Friends of James River Park. Dine inside or on the spacious outdoor deck. (Even though the Floodwall obscures an actual view of the river, the ambience is still there.)

Jocelyn Carrillo and Kii Johnson, students at Matoaka High School, pose for this photo on the Tyler Potterfield Memorial Bridge. Kii enjoys biking throughout the James River Park System.

Great Shiplock Park & Chapel Island

With its entrance at the intersection of Dock and Pear Streets, the family-friendly Great Shiplock Park (part of Chapel Island) showcases the downstream-most historic lock that allowed boats to enter the system of canals and locks through which they would transport goods through the seven-mile "falls" section of the James River and then onto the main river and canals farther upstream for nearly 200 miles west. The Park's features include a parking lot for 25 cars (always full on weekends and many afternoons), a small bay in which persons swim and fish, a launch into the river for non-motorized boats, fishing in the canal and lock, a wooded trail, a secluded picnic table, and interpretive signage about history and nature.

Among the more notable historic features are the remnants of the Trigg Shipbuilding Company that produced torpedo boats and destroyers using 2,000 employees and 15 buildings on Chapel Island during the turn of the 20th Century. President William McKinley was present for the launch of the first ship — a 175-foot torpedo boat — which was witnessed by 30,000 spectators. The company built two dozen more boats before Trigg died in 1903.

The Park also features a section of the Virginia Capital Trail that proceeds east all the way to Jamestown, and west for a few blocks to its trailhead at 17th Street. ≈

▼ PICTURED BELOW, LEFT: Petersburg residents Lucifer Gray and Laura Johnson enjoy fishing in the lock at Great Shiplock Park. Lucifer is a writer of horror/suspense (Poe is his favorite), and Laura is a manager for Food Lion. I asked Lucifer if he has gotten any writing ideas while here: "Yes, (long pause) about what's on the end of her line." Laura raised her eyebrows and smiled.

Mechanics Tom Robinson and Mark Harrison love launching at Huguenot Flatwater and paddling to Bosher's Dam where they can relax on an island and then enjoy a leisurely float back. Tom especially enjoys early morning outings when he can see the sunrise.

Huguenot Flatwater

With its entrance and 35-car parking area located at 8600 Southampton Road just a short walk upstream from the Huguenot Bridge, this 37-acre section of the James River Park System has a wonderful "universal access" ramp for launching canoes, kayaks, and tubes; and wooded walking trails with side-path access to shoreline fishing. At river levels below 5 feet the river is absent of dangerous rapids from here all the way upstream to Bosher's Dam, thus providing an enjoyable opportunity for paddlers of all skill levels. **CAUTION: If you go downstream you will soon encounter dangerous rapids and hydraulics.** ≈

How to Tie Down a Boat to a Sedan Without Roof Racks!

There's a great little video that shows how. Just go to **rvapaddlesports.com**. At the bottom of the landing page under Quick Links, click on Boat & Gear Rentals.

The Low Line

Situated below a trestled, active railroad, the Low Line is an urban green space and walkway that stretches west from Great Shiplock Park, located at Dock and Pear Streets, to the Richmond Floodwall at 17th Street, mostly along the Kanawha Canal. Regularly sprinkled with cyclists, joggers, and walkers, the Low Line is a popular destination for recreation, relaxation, and even fishing on the bank of the canal. Plus, it serves as the western end of the Virginia Capital Trail. The Low Line is immersed in the history of tobacco sale, shipbuilding, slave trade, and hallmark events such as Lincoln's visit to Richmond on April 4, 1864, after its capture by the Union. Thanks to the nonprofit organization, Capital Trees, the Low Line is beautifully flowered and landscaped. ≈

▼PICTURED BELOW, LEFT: The Low Line maintains its landscaping beauty thanks to persons like volunteer Julie H. (left) and Capital Trees horticultural consultant Mary Petres, who owns a landscaping business.

North Bank Park

aka Texas Beach

The stairwell that leads down from the train track bridge at the North Bank section of James River Park is filled with bright murals painted years ago under the direction of Ruth Bolduan and Michael Royce.

The entrance to this wonderfully wooded wilderness with a 35-car parking lot is at 1941 Texas Avenue. There is a down-to-the-river path composed of wooden steps, a footbridge across railroad tracks, dirt trail, and a planked walkway across a sometimes wet lowland. Side trails lead both upstream and downstream. One of the bonuses of the hike down to the river is the group of colorful murals painted on the walls of the stairwell of the railroad bridge. The area's primary attractions are its relative seclusion and its calm waters that are great for wading and swimming. Its past-years sketchy reputation has now been eclipsed by the presence of all sorts of park-goers including families with children. On weekends the parking lot fills quickly, but there is abundant street parking throughout the neighborhood. First-time visitors will learn that the hike down to the river is a bit longer than expected — but well worth it. ≈

▶PICTURED RIGHT, 2ND FROM TOP: Ally Johnson and 3-year-old Skylar Rose Hutchinson walk the trail from Texas Beach after an unexpected rainburst.

▶PICTURED RIGHT, BOTTOM: RPS social worker Erin Callahan, her uncle Tony Reichhardt who lives in Fredericksburg and is a retired editor of *Smithsonian Air and Space Magazine*, and her son Cash Callahan, enjoy an afternoon at Texas Beach.

The Pipeline

View of the Pipeline Overlook from below on the Pipeline.

The Pipeline, located along the north side of the river just upstream from the 14th Street Bridge, and accessed on a trail leading downstream from the Pipeline Overlook (Byrd and 12th Streets) or through Floodwall "doors" located 150 yards downstream from the Overlook, is one of those areas that is only appreciated when experienced in person. It's one of the least accessible areas of the river, requiring climbing down a 6-foot metal ladder, walking along a handrailed narrow catwalk (barely wide enough for two persons to pass one another), and atop a narrow NON-railed pipe. But the views are spectacular: the river's most challenging rapids, boulders and rocks and islands and the "Devil's Kitchen" area. The Pipeline's feeling of seclusion and secrecy is enhanced by the cave-like atmosphere that results from its "ceiling" of overhead railroad tracks. Once you climb down and onto the Pipeline, there is a metal catwalk of approximately 300 yards that then transitions to walking directly atop the concrete-encased pipeline for another 250 yards until transitioning onto a trail upstream along the river. Early along the metal catwalk is a sandy area — climb-downable for the nimble — that invites swimming and wading and relaxation. There are additional areas upstream

Mike and Vivian Flynn, whose business is RVA4Wellness, host grandson Parker Flynn, who lives in Charlottesville, for his first visit to the Pipeline

▲PICTURED ABOVE: Canadians April Harris and Haywood Krodel, first-time visitors to the urban James, prepare to walk through the Floodwall to see the Pipeline.

that, with careful footing, can accommodate wading and shallow swimming. Birders will enjoy the Pipeline's springtime nesting of Great Blue Herons, and anglers will enjoy the Pipeline's proximity to relatively undisturbed fishing spots. ≈

▲ PICTURED ABOVE: Christine and Eric Patterson and children Aiden (3) and Gavin (2), pictured here at Pony Pasture, have enjoyed many areas along the urban James including Robious Landing Park which is near their home. When asked about fun activities for families with little children, their simultaneous answer was, "Picnics!"

Pony Pasture

Located at 7200 Riverside Drive, Pony Pasture is an extremely popular, family-friendly segment of the James River Park System, and its 100-car parking lot always fills fast on good-weather weekends. The area offers wooded hike/bike trails; a launch for canoes, kayaks and float tubes; lots of boulders and flat rocks for relaxing; plenty of non-rapid pools for wading, swimming and snorkeling; Class II rapids that see a continual flow of watercraft; wonderful views for photography; and great fishing for anglers who are willing to wade and rock-hop away from the crowds. And of course Pony Pasture is a great place to observe wildlife and birds — especially at dawn. The area was named because of its use as a privately-owned pasture where ponies were kept in the 1960s. ≈

Visitors from California — Kenney Reeves who does post production for reality television, and Alex Dell'Amico who works in real estate - have discovered Richmond's urban James River and have decided that they would love to have their wedding (planned for 2023) right here.

Corey Allen, owner of a tequila company and resident of Virginia Beach, enjoys fishing when visiting cousins in Richmond.

Pump House Park

(friendsofpumphouse.org)

Pump House Park, located at 1799 Pump House Drive and with plenty of street parking and bike racks, has a wooded walking trail, the first canal lock system in the nation, a canal ramp for kayaks and canoes, fishing opportunities, picnic table, and the historic 1880s Pump House that was not only a pumping station but also a venue for lavish events until the mid-1920s. Now in long non-use and disrepair, the building is open only for guided tours and carefully planned events. Visitors can view and see interpretive signage for three historic canals, two granite canal locks, and an 18th Century archway celebrating a visit from George Washington. ≈

IMPORTANT WARNING: There is no legal access to the James River from Pump House Park, even though persons routinely cut passage through the wire fencing and illegally (and dangerously) traverse the adjacent railroad tracks to get to the river.

▶ PICTURED RIGHT: Charleston, WV native Penn Markham, an electrical engineer for Dominion Energy, and President of Friends of Pump House, moved to Richmond from Knoxville. He loves Richmond, especially the city's variety of historic architecture.

▼ PICTURED BELOW: Because of its seclusion and lesser crowds, Pump House Park is the favorite part of the James River Park System of Sam Shields and Lily Watts. Sam is an art history major at Bard College (Donald Judd is one of his favorites) and Lily is a multi-media artist.

PUMPHOUSE · 3 MILE LOCK P

PRIMARY FEATURES OF THIS PAR
ARE THE 19TH CENTURY PUMPHOU
CANALS CONSTRUCTED IN THE 18
CENTURY, EARLY AND LATE 19T
CENTURY AND RELATED CANAL LOC
BY ITS HISTORIC NATURE
THIS PARK IS CHARACTERIZ
BY STEEP BANKS, UNEVEN GRO
OPEN WATER AND VERTICAL WALLED L
SMALL CHILDREN MUST BE CAREFULLY ATTE

STAY OFF THE TRACKS!

Years ago I met and talked with Andrew Mangum, Special Agent with the Police Department for CSX for 18 years, who was spending much of his time apprehending persons who trespass on the railroad tracks along Richmond's James River. He told me that Pump House Park is one of the top five trespassing areas in the region. "One of the worst things people do is crawl through the drawheads (where the couplers are) on stopped trains." Without warning the train can jerk or lurch and cause a fatality. He told me that the CSX system, that covers many states, averages two to three fatalities per week.

Reedy Creek

The Reedy Creek entrance to the James River Park System is at the intersection of Hillcrest and Riverside and has a 25-car parking lot. The area's main feature is the highly-used canoe/kayak ramp located where Reedy Creek empties into one of the river's side channels. Knowledge of the navigation route is necessary to reach the main river.

The area is also the site of the headquarters building of the James River Park System, a meadow with a variety of plant and insect life, picnic table, bike rack, water fountain, restroom, both-direction access to the Buttermilk Trail, and a popular biking/walking gravel road that leads downstream to Belle Isle. **Note:** This area's barrier of thin channels and islands blocks it from the main river, and thus there are no ideal areas for swimming or wading. But the area is very popular with bikers and hikers.

The Silber family, Andrew (firefighter), Erin (physical therapist) and triplets (l-r) Kieran, Mira, and Cillian, pictured here at the James River Park System Headquarters, love all of the trails. The triplets love finding sticks and throwing rocks into the water. Andrew and Erin moved to RVA from New Jersey 8 years ago and love the Park. "We're here all the time!"

Requests from Giles Garrison, Superintendent, James River Park System

❶ Leave nothing but footprints; take nothing but photos.

❷ Be our eyes and ears in the Park; let us know if there are concerns: (804) 646-6443.

❸ Bring a newbie to the Park.

◄ PICTURED LEFT: Abbie Ceneviva, Controller for Taylor & Parrish, and children Felicity (6), Kendall (8), and Asher (1), seen here at the Reedy Creek entrance, enjoy biking throughout the James River Park including Belle Isle, Brown's Island, the Canal Walk, T. Tyler Potterfield Memorial Bridge, etc.

▲ PICTURED ABOVE, LEFT IMAGE: Elizabeth Guilamo (front) and Skylar, Ava and Andre Green are part of the 50-person Austin Family Reunion gathered at Robious Landing. Andre, who worked at RVA's airport until 1992, works at Dallas Loveland Airport. Elizabeth's job is cleaning subways in New York City; she says she's found some interesting things. The lower photo on the t-shirts is of Andre's late father, Albert Green, Jr., who started the Austin Family Reunion.

Robious Landing Park

Robious Landing Park, located at 3800 James River Road, and with a 92-car parking lot, provides a nice ramp for non-motorized watercraft. A popular river access for kayaking, canoeing, paddleboarding, rowing, and even swimming from the floating dock, the 102-acre site also has 3.4 miles of wooded trails — including a 1.5-mile graveled trail that is highly accessible and a 27-species tree ID trail — a floating dock, playgrounds, picnic shelters and sand volleyball.

Birders enjoy water-oriented species including osprey, bald eagles, red-shouldered hawks, great blue herons, and kingfishers, as well as woodland species such as flycatchers, warblers, vireos, woodpeckers and barred owls, and also grassland species such as bluebirds and robins. Anglers along this flatwater section of the river catch smallmouth and largemouth bass, bluegill, redbreast sunfish, channel catfish, and gar. One caution for paddlers is that fast motorized boats use this section of the river. ≈

▼ PICTURED BELOW, LEFT IMAGE: Greg (Final Gravity Brewing), Leandra (DOD contractor), and Lilian (age 1 1/2) Rolf enjoy much of the urban James, and especially love the Robious Landing area because of the easy access that the ramp and floating dock provide for kayaks and paddleboards.

Rocketts Landing Wharf

▲ PICTURED ABOVE:
Antoinette (insurance sales) and Timothy (crawlspace medic) Horton release most of the fish that they catch here at the dock area on the north side of the river across from Ancarrow's Landing.

L ocated along Wharf Street just east of downtown Richmond and just west of the Rocketts Landing residential community, this site was named for Robert Rockett who ran a ferry across the river beginning in the 1730s. Today it's a 250-yard-long concrete wharf that is used mostly for fishing. (The wharf is too high above the water for swimming or boating access.) Paralleling the edge of the tidal river, and providing immediate parking for 50 cars, this is by far the easiest and most accessible fishing location on the urban James. Catfish are the predominant species except for during the month of April when this part of the river fills with shad, stripers, white perch and other species. The western portion, at the end of which was located the city's Municipal Wharf, is bordered by a grassy field that families often use for picnics and relaxation. ≈

ROCKETTS LANDING
★ ★ ★
Confederate Navy Yard

Yoga on the wharf.

Jack Maher is one of the owners of Sea Suite Cruises which offers a unique Paddle Boat Cruise opportunity out of Rocketts Landing. Groups from 16-20 persons bring their own beverages and socialize while eating, drinking, and peddling (or not) at 16 peddle stations that propel the boat's stern paddlewheel. The boat also has an engine that is engaged as necessary. Reservations only: www.seasuitecruises.com

ROCKETTS LANDING

Rocketts, or Rocketts Landing, is the river frontage of the community, named for Robert Rockett who operated a ferry across the James River beginning in the 1730s. Tenant laborers and merchants filled the floodplain with clusters of small houses and commerical establishments. Free black residents, Jews, and immigrants from Germany, Scotland, and Ireland worked to make Rocketts a prosperous world seaport between 1790 and 1830. Shipping lines connected Rocketts to Philadelphia, New York, Charleston, and various South American and European ports. Tobacco and flour were the main exports. Between 1830 and 1861 Rocketts became more of a manufacturing center for tobacco products than a bulk shipping center.

Rocketts Landing Residential Community

At 4708 Old Main Street, on the edge of Richmond's city limits, Rocketts Landing is today an upscale residential development with streets, restaurants, boat slips, pools, beach volleyball, and more — all overlooking the river: "Richmond's riverfront neighborhood. Home to families, professionals, restaurants, businesses, herons and bald eagles. Come here for dinner, kayaking or a miles-long bike ride." Although most of the boat slips are for private rental, there are a few that are available for $5 for boaters who want to tie up and have a meal at one of the restaurants. AND, the Virginia Capital Trail goes right through Rocketts Landing overlooking the river. ≈

▼ PICTURED BELOW: Arlington native and VCU business and communications student Jack Durham works for Freedom Boat Club that offers rental boats at Rocketts Landing (www.freedomboatclub.com). Jack loves the James River Park System: "Incredibly beautiful, and so much history."

▼ PICTURED BELOW: Northern Virginia native Ryan Tomajczyk, dockmaster for Rocketts Landing, began working at Rocketts 15 years ago. The rental boat slips are usually full from spring through fall, but develop new openings in the winter. There are 15 public slips — available for $5 for a few hours (convenient for boaters who want to enjoy one of Rocketts' restaurants).

HONOR BOX DOCKING FEE $5~2 HOURS OR LESS

Tredegar Beach

Tredegar Beach is the popular name for the sandy area that is nestled between the headgate of the Kanawha Canal, railroad pillars, and the Tredegar Street put-in/take-out. Located along Tredegar Street just opposite the American Civil War Museum, Tredegar Beach is an extremely popular spot with all ages for swimming, relaxing, and playing in the sand. Plus, it's close to Brown's Island, Belle Isle, the Canal Walk, etc. The adjacent put-in/take-out is used daily by paddlers of all skills to enjoy the calm waters in the immediate area, and by skilled paddlers coming from the challenging upriver rapids and going to the challenging downriver rapids. ≈

▼ PICTURED BELOW, MIDDLE IMAGE: Daughter Crystal Robertson and mother Pamela Robertson shared smiling reminiscences about good times here at Tredegar Beach. "My grandbabies used to swim and play here," said Pamela, a Bank of America retiree. Crystal works for the Department of Justice.

T. Tyler Potterfield Memorial Bridge
aka T-Pott Bridge

This 500-yard footbridge, readily accessible from the southern side of Brown's Island, is a must-experience opportunity to view the river in its full glory: its rapids, its water birds and raptors, its panorama juxtaposed against downtown's office buildings, its historic bridge remnants, etc.

The bridge is just perfect in that it's simultaneously wide enough for both bicycles and pedestrians, its side-fencing is safe without being visually obstructive, its walkway is firm-footed and secure, and its length is long enough for good exercise and short enough to not be off-putting. You'll see every slice of life on this bridge, from babies in back- and front-packs, to prime-of-youth exuberance, to old-age slow-walkers. And in the river, just a few feet below, you'll see kayakers and tubers and paddleboarders and even occasional anglers.

Perched atop remnants of a 1900 concrete dam used for hydroelectric power, the T-Pott Bridge connects the southern and northern shores of the river. At the south end of the bridge, you'll see the adjacent Manchester Wall and

▲ PICTURED ABOVE: Assemblies of God pastor Nathan Jones and wife, counselor Brittany Jones, grew up in RVA and have enjoyed the urban James all their lives — especially the T-Pott Bridge and the trails.

JC Gilmore-Bryan, Angelina Hines, and Kate Flippin walking the T-Pott.

▲ PICTURED ABOVE, LEFT IMAGE: Liz and Bob Blue, and Catherine and John McSorley enjoy running, paddleboarding, biking, etc. along Richmond's urban James. As this photo was taken on the T-Pott Bridge, they were getting ready to watch their children participate in Dominion Energy Riverrock's kayak competition in the rapids just behind them.

its accompanying pillars which are regional and national rock-climbing destinations.

Here is some of what is said on the website of Friends of James River Park: "A student of architecture, Tyler Potterfield came to Richmond in 1991 and became one of our staunchest advocates of documenting and preserving Richmond's history. In examining how our city's society was stratified around the James River, he became even more of an advocate for linking the James River Park to our future. Many of the ideas and initiatives we discuss about the James River Park Master Plan came from the mind of Potterfield. One of his goals

was to connect more visitors to the James River Park. And the bridge named in his honor is a fitting example of that. While there are many areas to leisurely splash in the James, some might bore the adventurous kayaker. Many of the trails that are exciting for mountain bikes may frustrate the casual walker. But the Potterfield Bridge offers a bridge for all."

As you walk onto the bridge from Brown's Island you'll see underfoot a permanent history installation entitled "Three Days in April 1865." You'll walk over 21 metal planks that provide quotations from Richmond's final days as the capital of the Confederacy. ≈

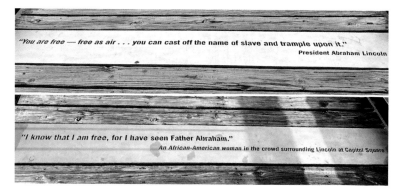

Virginia Capital Trail

(virginiacapitaltrail.org)

This is the 51.7-mile bike/run/walk/skateboard family-friendly paved trail that runs from Richmond to Jamestown (and vice versa). The western trailhead is in downtown Richmond where South 17th Street meets the Floodwall, and is beautifully gardened and manicured and sprinkled with well-designed interpretive signage about the area's historic significance. From there it goes 1.3 miles east along the Kanawha Canal and the James River, including through Great Shiplock Park, and later enters Rocketts Landing as it exits Richmond city limits. ≈

Start exploring the trail.

▼PICTURED BELOW, LEFT IMAGE: Getting ready to start the Virginia Capital Trail at Great Shiplock Park, Chris Graves doesn't have enough time to do the entire trail, but hopes to complete at least 20 miles. A financial portfolio manager in Northern Virginia, Chris has known about the Trail, but this is his first time on it.

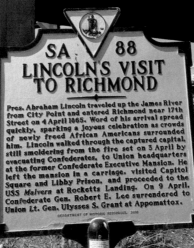

SA 88
LINCOLN'S VISIT
TO RICHMOND

Pres. Abraham Lincoln traveled up the James River from City Point and entered Richmond near 17th Street on 4 April 1865. Word of his arrival spread quickly, sparking a joyous celebration as crowds of newly freed African Americans surrounded him. Lincoln walked through the captured capital, still smoldering from the fire set on 3 April by evacuating Confederates, to Union headquarters at the former Confederate Executive Mansion. He left the mansion in a carriage, visited Capitol Square and Libby Prison, and proceeded to the USS *Malvern* at Rocketts Landing. On 9 April, Confederate Gen. Robert E. Lee surrendered to Union Lt. Gen. Ulysses S. Grant at Appomattox.

DEPARTMENT OF HISTORIC RESOURCES, 2010

51.2

VIRGINIA
CAPITAL TRAIL

Richmond Riverfront

Noah Kelly (20) and Cinnamon (4) are travelers who were last in New York and will soon depart for California. Noah, currently saving money to buy a school bus, is a craftsman: formerly tie-dyed shirts, and forthcoming walking sticks.

Physical therapist Janell Edwards enjoys sunbathing at her favorite spot along the urban James.

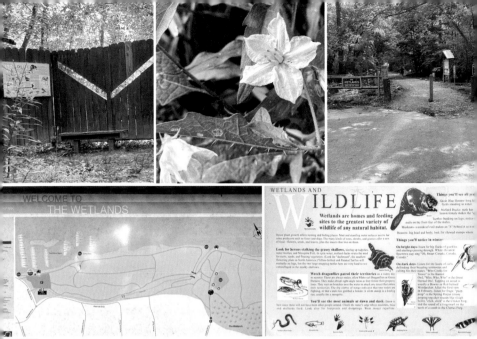

The Wetlands

Located at the end of Landria Drive, and with a "lot" that holds 8 cars and street parking for another 20 cars, this lusciously wooded area offers trails and also a shallow pond that has blinds from which to observe wildlife. Swimming and wading are somewhat accessible here along the trail, but boating is not readily accessible. But if you like walking in the woods and enjoying nature, you'll love this part of the James River Park. The main trail is highly wheelchair-accessible with some assistance. ≈

Fireflies

In 2022 (and hopefully in future years) the Virginia Chapter of the Sierra Club offered a "Firefly Foray" on Friday evenings in June, hosted by Ralph White at the Wetlands section of James River Park. "The light show is amazing; it looks like there are millions of flashing green Christmas lights in the tree canopies. You will see green, yellow, white, blue, and red lights, all with different trajectories and blinking patterns."

Williams Island

Slightly less than 100 acres, and located approximately 300 yards north and across the river from Pony Pasture, Williams Island can be reached only by boat or by wading/swimming. The forested island, popular with anglers, is rich with flora (more than 200 species of plants) and fauna (lots of birds, river otter, deer, fox, raccoon, muskrat, skunk, turkey, snakes, turtles, and more). There are no man-made artifacts or construction, and because the island is low and flat it is routinely subject to immersion by high water. You can find explorations of the island on YouTube. ≈

PLACES

14th Street Takeout

The 14th Street Takeout's official address is 1601 East Byrd Street, but that's misleading. If you're headed south towards the river on 14th Street, turn left immediately after you pass the Floodwall. (It's common to miss the turn unless you know it's there.) The lot has room for 20 cars and signage says that parking is reserved for vehicles equipped for carrying canoes and kayaks.

Highly used by skilled paddlers, this is the primary put-in and take-out on the downstream border of Richmond and has a wonderful ramp in a side-channel of the river. Flatwater paddlers can use this for immediate access to the tidal portion of the river. And anglers are often found fishing from the shoreline. When departing this area by car, be careful. There is usually plenty of traffic and it's difficult to see what's coming. ≈

▲ PICTURED ABOVE: Left to Right: Bailey Gillespy, a VCU graduate student from Florida; Jen Jimenez, a manager for Riverside Outfitters; and Jen Skrzypek, a realtor from Pennsylvania; preparing to depart from the river at the 14th Street Takeout.

14th St. Takeout

These steps to the river provide the first official Parks Department take out point for boaters who have just run the finest urban white water in the nation. They were built in the Fall of 2005 with major funding and labor from the James Outdoor Coalition and the Friends of James River Park System under the supervision of James River Park Staff members Peter, Bruce, and Nathan Burrell. The land was a generous gift from the Department of Public Utilities.

This River Access is the latest episode in a 300 year tradition of urban use along the James River. It contains the traces of early residential and commercial development as well as the unmistakable signs of increasing recreational use and environmental stewardship. Here is a unique opportunity to see how Richmond used the riverfront in the past and how it embraces the river today.

D'Vonte Waler, former quarterback for state champion Highland Springs High School and now quarterback at Virginia State University, fishes most days in the summer — mostly at the 14th Street Takeout.

Additional contributions provided by Richmond Whitewater Club, Transit Lumber Falls Prime Company, and Coastal Canoeists. Sign paid for by a donation from the James River.

35 | THE JAMES RIVER IN RICHMOND: YOUR NEW GUIDE

22ⁿᵈ Street Entrance

▼PICTURED BELOW: The family here at the 22ⁿᵈ Street Entrance to James River Park are tourists. The son (left) lives in Delaware and his parents are visitors from India. (They gave permission for this photo but preferred not to provide their names.)

This entrance to James River Park is where 22ⁿᵈ Street meets Riverside and has a parking lot that can accommodate more than 30 cars. It has access to the Buttermilk Trail which goes both up- and downriver. Downriver the trail quickly arrives at the 21ˢᵗ Street tower that crosses a bridge over the railroad, and then down a stairwell. The trail then continues downriver to the Dry Rocks area and further to a bridge to Belle Isle. At the northeast corner of the 22ⁿᵈ Street parking area you'll see a trail leading up granite steps, but take that route only if you enjoy very difficult footing. The alternate and easy-footing downstream trail is accessed on the east side of the drive that enters the parking lot. The two routes merge at the 21ˢᵗ Street tower. The 22ⁿᵈ Street Entrance is used by persons who enjoy hiking or biking a fairly long distance through wooded trails, and by persons who enjoy the Dry Rocks section of the river. ≈

Riverglass

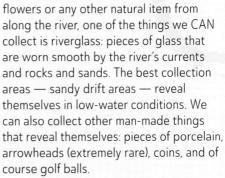

Although we don't take rocks or driftwood or flowers or any other natural item from along the river, one of the things we CAN collect is riverglass: pieces of glass that are worn smooth by the river's currents and rocks and sands. The best collection areas — sandy drift areas — reveal themselves in low-water conditions. We can also collect other man-made things that reveal themselves: pieces of porcelain, arrowheads (extremely rare), coins, and of course golf balls.

42nd Street

This wonderful access to James River Park is located at 4401 Riverside Drive, where 42nd Street meets Riverside. There is a parking lot that holds 34 cars. From the lot it's a downhill trek to the river, and it includes a treetop bridge that crosses railroad tracks — a great area for birdwatching. At the bottom of the bridge's stairwell are wooded pathways that lead upriver, downriver, and directly toward the river across a bouldered creek and through poison-ivy-sprinkled woods.

▼PICTURED BELOW: Intent on moving from California to the southeast a few years ago, Kyle McCann, a marketing professional with Smith Optics, considered a handful of cities, and his visit to RVA and the James River Park System sealed the deal. He especially enjoys fishing (a "rod agnostic" but leans towards the fly rod when possible) and cycling (a "bike agnostic" — both gravel and mountain). After moving to RVA, he and his girlfriend (now wife) "spent every morning walking the fire road on Reedy Creek down to the 42nd Street island entrance" which was so inspirational that "I proposed on the rocks crossing to the island at 42nd Street."

Angelina Hines at 42nd Street stairway.

All along the river are inviting boulder-strewn places to rock-hop, wade, swim, sunbathe, fish, and simply relax. And there are sandy areas where you can find shells of various clams and mussels and snails. Careful searching will reveal other types of river-washed debris such as riverglass and river ceramic, including an occasional piece that is quite old.

This part of the James River Park System is a favorite area for seclusion as well as enjoying abundant flora and fauna. The area is accessible only to persons who have adequate agility to negotiate rocks and boulders as well as the initial steep downhill steps and the railroad bridge stairwell. ≈

◄PICTURED LEFT, BOTTOM IMAGE: Richmond native Cydney Oleniacz, an AmeriCorps Service Member assigned to Richmond Department of Parks & Recreation, is project manager for the "Riverside Relationships Mural" that is painted on and in the stairwell at the 42nd Street Entrance to James River Park. The mural, painted by the TRIP (Teens of Richmond In Parks) program, depicts native flora and fauna. Cydney, a painter and potter who graduated from VCU's School of the Arts, has a special interest in native plants.

Timmons Group project engineer Laura Hamilton, Kelly Driglia of CapTech Consulting, and medical student Mary Alice Strohmeyer, seen here with their dog Kai, enjoy virtually all areas of the urban James.

Activities & Interests

There are dozens, perhaps even hundreds, of distinct activities and interests that persons pursue along Richmond's James River. This section of this guidebook provides information on the ones that are most popular. But I welcome readers' advice regarding additional entries for a future edition of this book: jbryanfish@aol.com.

Local buskers Raymon Harris, Lynard Wright and Lorenzo Brooks — seen here on a gateway street to the annual Dominion Energy Riverrock, have been together as street buskers for over 10 years. Their percussion is freestyle, and new techniques emerge daily. Their YouTube site is Bukithedz.

Trails for Foot & Wheel

▲PICTURED ABOVE: Travis Hall, Product Manager for the Portland, Oregon-headquartered Stages Cycling, moved to RVA from Portland and continues to work remotely. He is a huge fan of the cycling trails along the James River. When asked his opinion of the Skills Area on Belle Isle he smiled and replied, "It's GREAT!" He is pictured here with his son, Julian, and you can see more of them by Googling Travis Hall Stages Cycling.

There are more than 22 miles of hike/bike trails along the Richmond portion of the James River — some trails that traverse luscious woods with abundant flora and fauna, some that encounter significant historical sites and structures, and others that include flat, open areas. The trails are subject to continual maintenance, improvement, and amenities — much of this provided by volunteers and nonprofit organizations.

There are four basic guidelines for use of the trails.

❶ Cyclists should be courteous and announce themselves when overtaking others.

❷ Earbuds are discouraged for all users of the trails.

❸ Dogs must be kept on leashes.

❹ Don't use the trails when they are wet or muddy; such use damages them.

Google and you'll find several websites that provide daily reports on RVA trail conditions. And/or find conditions on Twitter and/or Instagram: **@rvatrailreport #dailytrailreport**

Following are descriptions of the main trails. The parts that are in quotation marks are taken from the website of Friends of James River Park **(jamesriverpark.org).** ≈

Buttermilk Trail (not wheelchair accessible)

The 2.5-mile Buttermilk Trail "parallels the south side of the river and is a real challenge and considered the most difficult of the different sections of the James River Park System. Buttermilk combines tight, twisty, fast descents and steep climbs with lots of rocks and roots. Several creek crossings and some bridges and rock gardens add character to one of the most beloved trail systems in the Richmond area." Buttermilk has three sections. Buttermilk East runs from the Manchester Bridge to 22nd street; Buttermilk Proper goes from 22nd Street to 43rd Street; and Buttermilk Heights, with the most rocks and climbing, extends from 43rd Street to the Boulevard Bridge. **Hikingproject.com** has a great description of the trail, condensed and paraphrased here:

You can enter the Buttermilk Trail at the 22nd Street Entrance to James River Park. The trail is to your left. It goes up and crosses a small creek. In around 300 yards the trail goes back downhill and you will encounter a small side trail on the right. This trail avoids a steep descent ahead. Bear right when you meet the main trail again. There will then be a rocky area followed by a newer area that has fewer obstacles and two wooden bridges. A bit later the trail forks. Stay right. (The left fork goes into Forest Hill Park.)

After bearing right and crossing a bridge the trail continues to the Reedy Creek parking lot and then enters the woods on the other side of the lot. In a fourth of a mile the trail continues up stairs and a ramp for bikers. This part of the trail passes three creeks and lots of roots that present challenges.

The trail ascends with switchbacks and four more bridges, then forks at the top of the hill. The left fork goes to the right side of the Boulevard Bridge. The right fork goes under the bridge to reach its left side. (You can cross the bridge to get to Pump House Drive, Pump House Park and the trailhead of the North Bank Trail.) ≈

North Bank Trail

(not wheelchair accessible)

The 2.5-mile North Bank Trail "is an advanced trail that is technical, rocky and rugged in spots. Fast, flowing singletrack with some steep climbs and fast descents — users should be careful of oncoming mountain bikers and pedestrians. This trail offers great panoramic views of the James River unavailable in other sections of the Park. The trail runs from the Boulevard Bridge (parking lot and trail entrance just off Pump House Drive) to Tredegar Iron Works parking lot (beneath the Lee Bridge)."

Mtbproject.com has a great description of the trail, condensed and paraphrased here:

Richmonders Stu and Tobias Ross (9) preparing to traverse the North Bank Trail on onewheels. Stu, a cannabis growth consultant, also enjoys surfboarding the standing waves in Belle Ilse's Hollywood Rapids.

The North Bank Trail travels between the parking lots for Belle Isle and Pump House Park. Enter the trail next to the kiosk in the Pump House parking lot on Pump House Drive. The trail proceeds below the Boulevard Bridge and crosses a creek and continues along a chain link fence, then merges onto a dirt road and a wooden ramp.

At the top of the ramp take the road and after three blocks turn right at a stop sign. (You will see North Bank Trail signs.) Then go one block to the North Bank Park parking lot and take the trail that continues straight making a right bend after the small wooden bridge creek crossing.

From here the trail is obvious, including a section that is split for bikers and hikers. The final part is via a dirt road at the bottom of a grass hill. Then turn right across a foot-access bridge down to the Belle Isle parking lot. ≈

Ancarrow's Landing Trail

(not wheelchair accessible)

The 2.5-mile Ancarrow's Landing Trail (aka Poop Loop because of its proximity to the Richmond Wastewater Treatment Plant) is a "twisty singletrack trail that starts at Ancarrow's Landing (at the end of Brander Street) and heads south to form a loop. It is very flat and suitable for beginner riders, but it is also one of the last trails to dry after a rain." ≈

Belle Isle Trails (main loop is wheelchair accessible)

Belle Isle (accessible via the Footbridge beneath the Lee Bridge) has approximately 3 miles of trails including the 1.2-mile flat, easy and accessible main loop. Narrower and more difficult tributary trails climb to the top of the island. "The Lost Trail is located on the eastern edge of the island, and is a flat, flowing trail with a few bermed turns. The other section is located on top of the hill in the middle of the island. Connecting these two trails is the Lost Garden, a long rock garden under the service bridge. The trails on top of the island's hill are moderately more difficult, with tight singletrack riddled with lots of roots and tight turns, with great views of the river near the western side of the island." ≈

▲ PICTURED ABOVE: Cerlisa Collins, writer and criminal justice student at ODU, and artist Sean Brooks have lived in Richmond all their lives but have only recently discovered the joys of the river. Cerlisa's book, *I Will Survive*, was published in 2021. (She was stabbed and shot; learn about it on YouTube.) Sean's golden PBK medallion stands for "Paint Brush King."

Historic Slave Trail
(mostly wheelchair accessible with assistance)

The easy 2.5-mile Historic Slave Trail starts at Ancarrow's Landing (at the end of Brander Street) and proceeds along a wooded upstream path until merging with the Floodwall Walk and then crossing the 14th Street Bridge and into downtown Richmond to the site of the historic Lumpkin's Jail. There is wonderful interpretive signage along the trail. ≈

Huguenot Flatwater Trail
(wheelchair accessible with assistance)

The easy, flat, 1.5-mile Huguenot Flatwater Trail begins at the Huguenot Flatwater parking lot (at Riverside Drive and Southampton Street) and proceeds downstream. "This well-shaded and well-marked wooded trail is very flat, making it tend to stay muddy for prolonged periods during wet weather." ≈

Pony Pasture Trails

(partly wheelchair accessible)

There are approximately 3 miles of trails at the Pony Pasture area (7200 Riverside Drive) of the James River Park System. The wooded trails are mostly wide and graveled and easy. This area is one of the most heavily used sections of the James River Park System. ≈

Wetlands Trails (main loop is wheelchair accessible)

The Wetlands (at the end of Landria Drive) has 2.5 miles of trails that range from narrow dirt to wide gravel — all through wooded flatland. This area is adjacent to the Pony Pasture area and the trails connect. ≈

The Loop

(not wheelchair accessible)

The LOOP, usually distanced at approximately 6.5 miles, is the grand loop that is made by connecting the North Bank Trail to the Buttermilk Trail via the Boulevard Bridge and either the Belle Isle Footbridge or the T. Tyler Potterfield Memorial Bridge. I highly recommend the wonderful walking description of the Loop, by Erin Gifford, along with photos, at this site: **gohikevirginia.com/james-river-park-loop**. It chronicles a first-time, 3-hour hike of the Loop and points out which forks to take and not to take, what things to look for (such as the bears at Maymont Park), where to sit and savor the views, info about Buttermilk Spring (that gave the Buttermilk Trail its name), and more. The photos alone are worth the visit to this website. ≈

Trail Resources

A great, basic map of the trails can be found at **www.rvamore.org.** The site provides elevations, difficulty rating, condition, popularity, and type of activity (e.g. hiking, biking, running, e-biking, adaptive biking, etc.).

Additional great info can be found on other websites such as **alltrails.com, trailforks. com, greatruns.com, hikingproject.com,** etc. And you can find good videos on YouTube. For example, here's the link to a nice video of a first-time mountain bike ride on the singletrack Ancarrow's East Trail: **youtube.com/ watch?v=t57QB1DNPxl** ≈

▲ PICTURED ABOVE: Bryce Wilk, former Park Superintendent for the City of Richmond, is now Virginia State Park Central District Manager

Smiling Suggestions from
Alex Dahm

Venture Richmond's Operations Manager for Riverfront Canal Cruises and avid participant in all of the river's activities, Alex Dahm suggests the following:

1 Go up to folks and introduce yourself; people want to share the love.

2 Try everything. It's accessible at all levels.

3 Explore; there are so many detours in and out of the James River Park. Curious about something? Check it out!

4 The river is ours; take care of it.

Real estate attorney Carly and son Levin Nino enjoy biking on riverside trails — seen here beneath the Manchester Bridge.

Mountain Bike Drops

For great video instruction on how to mountain bike downhill over ledges and drops, go to rvamore.org and click on "Riding — Basic Skills" under the heading "Trails." You'll arrive at a group of instructive videos — the last of which is about "drops."

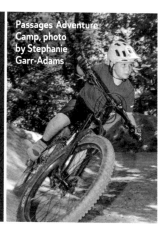

Passages Adventure Camp, photo by Stephanie Garr-Adams

Bicycle Safety

On a sunny Sunday afternoon on Belle Isle I encountered a fallen bicycle and bloody cyclist and introduced myself to injured Eric Fisher and good Samaritan Stephen Rice. Eric, a student at Christopher Newport University, had flown too high over a graveled hump in the large entrance field — "my first crash in years." Stephen, who runs an ambulance company in Virginia Beach, was nearby and had supplies in his bag. I watched as he cleaned and disinfected bloody scrapes, and then as he held up a finger and asked Eric to follow it with his eyes, and then as he examined a scraped spot on the top of Eric's head — a spot that was accompanied by lots of sheared hair. Stephen was successful in getting a bottle of water from a passerby — water for Eric to drink and to clean his head wound. The head bump concerned him, so he called for an ambulance and committed to staying with Eric until its arrival. Before I departed I asked Eric if he had any advice for others who bike in the James River Park System: "Wear a helmet and know your limits" — neither of which he'd done on this occasion.

Paddling, Floating & River Routes

The bucket list of every person, able-bodied or not, should include a trip down the James River's Richmond section — from the calm water near the Huguenot Bridge to the tidal boundary just past the 14th Street Bridge. The route ranges from calm meditation to wide-eyed exhilaration, from wooded-shoreline wilderness to business-district skyline, and always includes unexpected surprises. There is no entry fee to get on the river, and you don't have to make a reservation.

But there are of course safety considerations. Unless you're an experienced paddler, you shouldn't traverse the areas with rapids. And never ever traverse the rapids in non-professional inflatables such as inner tubes and swimming pool rafts. Those types of inflatables aren't rated for rapids and are impossible to propel and steer. Every year there are rescues of inexperienced paddlers and non-professional floaters. And sadly, there are occasional fatalities. Persons who launch giant rafts with big coolers usually have no idea what they're getting into and are flirting with disaster. (But one note: non-professional tubing from Huguenot Flatwater to Pony Pasture is usually okay but you MUST walk around the Z-Dam on the trail built on the shoreline of Williams Island!) And if you're going to go through rapids,

▲ PICTURED ABOVE: Husband/wife Mahum Nadeem, a physician at VCU, and Ammar Rashid, a mechanical engineer, originally from Pakistan, moved to RVA from San Francisco. This is their first time on the urban James.

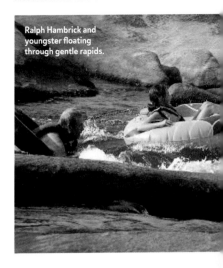

Ralph Hambrick and youngster floating through gentle rapids.

you should wear a personal floatation device and a helmet — and never go alone; always have a partner boat.

A vital consideration is the water level as measured at Westham Gauge (lots of websites for this, just Google James River Westham Gauge). At 5 feet and below, the river runs at its "normal" flow. But with every foot above 5 feet, the river's currents and rapids become increasingly more challenging. Personal floatation devices are recommended above 5 feet, and above 9 feet only expert paddlers should be on the river. The river level can rise quickly — as much as a couple of feet in a couple of hours. Upstream rain causes the river to rise, so be aware of rain from Goochland to Lynchburg. Even if Richmond is dry, a multi-inch downpour in Lynchburg can raise the Richmond James several feet.

If you're new to paddling (kayaks, canoes, stand-up paddleboards), you should get some basic instruction from a professional. You can find opportunities for instruction, classes, camps, etc. in the COMPANIES AND ORGANIZATIONS section of this book. That section also has

opportunities for professional float trips.

And finally, before you set out on the river, you may want to view a few river outings on YouTube. There are lots of videos for all river conditions. One that will give you a startling look at the river's power is entitled, "Insane Kayaking on Flooded James River."

There are seven put-in/takeout sites on the urban James: the universal access ramp at Huguenot Flatwater, a much-used ramp/ steps at Pony Pasture, the accessible ramp at Reedy Creek, the launch area at Tredegar Beach, the 14th Street Takeout beneath the 14th Street Bridge, the access on the south side of the river beneath the 14th Street Bridge, and the access ramp at Great Shiplock Park. (See the PLACES section of this book for more information about those

Greg Velzy coasting the Pony Pasture launch steps.

sites.) Huguenot Flatwater offers just what the name implies: calm water. But challenging rapids await quickly downstream. Pony Pasture's launch is amid intermediate rapids. Reedy Creek's ramp is easily accessed by car, but if approaching it from the river, you'll need to watch for a sign on a tree directing you to a side channel on the right. Tredegar Beach is at an easily-located flatwater area beneath the Lee Bridge. The 14th Street Takeout is on the river's downstream left channel just below the 14th Street Bridge where the flatwater tidal portion of the river begins. The access ramp at Great Shiplock Park is a mile downriver in a small inlet on the left.

Following is a basic description of a preferred route (during normal water levels) down the river beginning at Huguenot Flatwater. It should be noted that the river is sprinkled with islands and boulders of all sizes as well as various manmade structures and thus there are continual choices for the paddler. The following directions are meant only as a general guide. The only way to be certain about the route is to accompany an experienced paddler.

Put in at Huguenot Flatwater. (If you care to, you can paddle calm water 2 miles upstream to Bosher's Dam.) When going downstream from Huguenot Flatwater you'll navigate through some small islands and then you'll see the 95-acre Williams Island on your left, but go to the right side of the island. However, DO NOT go to the right side of the river. You will need to carry around the Z-Dam via the portage trail built on the shoreline of Williams Island so you can avoid the dangerous hydraulics and fish-notch of the Z-Dam. There are large signs directing you to that portage trail.

Then in less than a mile you'll encounter the Class II Pony Pasture Rapids and the Pony Pasture access ramp on the right, after which is a mile-long

stretch of intermediate and calm water. In another mile or so you'll reach the Class II Powhite Ledges rapids across the entire river a couple of hundred yards prior to reaching the Powhite Bridge. At low water levels, go to the extreme left to pass under the Powhite Bridge, then return to the center of the river for Choo-Choo Rapids just after the beautiful arched Atlantic Coastline Railroad Bridge. After Choo Choo Rapids, when the water level is below 6 feet, stay to the right side of the island that is downstream (Coopers Island). On this route you'll also encounter a water pipeline that creates a small 20-inch waterfall to go over. If running waterfalls isn't your thing you can walk or float around this at the far left.

Then stay in the middle of the river as you travel under the Boulevard Bridge. Then in a couple of hundred yards you'll encounter the Class II Mitchell's Gut rapids. If you want to find a takeout ramp after Mitchell's Gut, stay to the right and in about 400 yards enter the river's side channel on the right and you'll see a white sign on a tree directing you to the Reedy Creek ramp.

If you want to continue downriver after Mitchell's Gut, stay in the middle of the river through some islands and you'll encounter flatwater that is backed up by Belle Isle's levees. Head for the upstream tip of Belle Isle, and just before you get there you'll see a shallow dam that has a break in it called First Break Rapids (Class II). Go through those rapids and travel along the left side of Belle Isle and you'll begin one of the most hazardous sections of the river. Advance scouting is highly recommended if you're not familiar with this section. Numerous boulders require quick decisions.

You'll enter the Class II Approach Rapids after which you'll encounter the Class IV (V at high water) Hollywood Rapids. (Just as at Pony Pasture, you're likely to see lots of folks relaxing on the boulders.) After Hollywood Rapids it's smooth water as you approach the Lee Bridge and its underhanging Footbridge. The Tredegar Beach takeout is on the left side of the river just past the Lee Bridge.

You'll soon reach the T. Tyler Potterfield Memorial Bridge — a footbridge just 20 feet above the water and that is usually populated with diverse persons on foot and wheel. You will look for the large Blue

Scenic Rivers sign that indicates which opening to go through as you start into the Class II-III Vepco Levee/Fish Ladder rapids. After these rapids you can either work far right to the Southside Rapids that are followed by the takeout beneath the 14th Street Bridge, or stay towards the left side of the river for the traditional route that leads to the Pipeline Rapids which, along with Hollywood Rapids, are the urban river's most challenging. After Pipeline Rapids the 14th Street Takeout will be on your left.

Paddle another mile downstream from either takeout and on the left side of the river you'll see a little inlet in which is the Great Shiplock Park put-in/takeout.

From Huguenot Flatwater to the 14th Street Takeout (and/or to Great Shiplock Park) is an amazing journey, but it can't be stressed enough that the river is extremely dangerous, even life-threatening, for inexperienced paddlers and non-professional floaters. And even though you can find videos and maps on the Internet, you still need to accompany someone with experience before going it alone. And, although it's possible to go the entire length in one outing, the multiple launch sites make it possible to do just one or more sections depending on interest, time, and skill level. Indeed, a good way to get acquainted with the river is to bite off one chunk at a time. ≈

Best-friend families, (left to right) Ann, Dani, and Leighton Ossont, visiting from South Carolina, and Eli, Emma, Emily and Elmer Ligh, lifelong Richmonders, enjoy a late summer afternoon on Belle Isle. Emily and Elmer (who claims to be the world's youngest person named Elmer) are physical therapists. The whole family visits the river often and especially enjoys the trails. Earlier on this day they searched for and found Paw Paw fruit on the North Bank Trail.

Q&A with Ralph Hambrick,
a long-time paddler on the urban James

Ralph Hambrick guiding a float trip through Hollywood Rapids.

Q: What are the paddling opportunities on the urban James?

A: Multiple and diverse is the short answer. There are opportunities for enjoyment for all skill levels in canoes, kayaks, rafts, and paddleboards.

Q: What are the differences in the sections of the river?

A: That is a really nice feature of the river. There are sections for all skill levels. The area at Huguenot Flatwater is great for beginners or anybody who wants to paddle flatwater. There are some rocks and current, but it is not swift at normal levels. You can put in and paddle upstream as far as Bosher's Dam and downstream as far as Williams Dam on either side of Williams Island. The intermediate section begins at Williams Dam or, for a convenient put-in a little farther downstream, at Pony Pasture. The

intermediate section has nothing beyond Class II rapids. It goes to Reedy Creek on the right side of the river. The more advanced section begins at Belle Isle — downstream from the Reedy Creek put-in.

Q: Talk about the challenges of Williams Dam.

A: Most persons carry their boats around the Z-dam on the left side, using the established portage trail that is marked with signage. This leads to a nice sandy beach for swimming and relaxing. Even experienced paddlers avoid running the dam, including the fish notch, due to the dangerous hydraulics that have claimed numerous lives over the years.

Ralph Hambrick and student.

Q: What advice do you have for beginners?

A: Take some lessons. Or you can just go on the river. The Huguenot Flatwater area is quite forgiving to beginners. But if you know some basics you'll be a lot more comfortable and have more fun.

Q: What if you are an experienced paddler, but are not familiar with the river?

A: The toughest part might be finding the Reedy Creek Takeout. It's behind an island, marked by a sign on the right side of the river shortly after Mitchell's Gut — a nice, long wave-train rapid. And the first time on the downtown section, it is a good idea to go with someone who knows the routes.

Q: Are there any particular cautions on the urban James?

A: If you are paddling within your skill level, there are no serious danger spots. The river has the remnants of lots of dams and historic structures, but they rarely cause a problem. Hollywood and Pipeline Rapids are rated as Class IV, so some skill is required.

Q: How difficult are Hollywood and Pipeline Rapids?

A: An experienced paddler can go through them without difficulty. As the water level gets higher, so does the force of the water and the level of danger and skill required. There is a world of difference between running those rapids at 3.5 feet and at 10 feet or higher. After about 8 feet the Pipeline becomes particularly treacherous because the force of the water begins to push boats toward and under the large pipe. At flood stage a boat-eating hole develops at the bottom of Pipeline Rapids.

Q: Can you paddle during low water?

A: The urban James can be paddled at all levels.

Q: Has anyone on the river ever caused you any trouble?

A: No, and I have seen all types of people in all areas of the river.

Q: Can you paddle in the winter?

A: Yes. Lots of people paddle year-round. But you should have proper equipment and clothing. The rule of thumb is that you should never go ON the water unless you're prepared to go IN the water. In the winter you should at least wear a wet suit, and preferably a dry suit.

Q: What are mistakes people make in rapids?

A: People often tend to quit paddling when going through a rapid. They leave the paddle out of the water or grab the side of the boat. You should keep the paddle in the water or you'll lose stability. Another mistake is not keeping the boat straight. If you get sideways you easily can catch a rock and flip. Getting sideways is often caused by waiting too late to start a turn. It is easy to underestimate how far in advance you need to begin a turn.

Q: Why do you enjoy paddling the James River in Richmond?

A: I enjoy paddling on both ends of the spectrum. On one end is the relaxation, getting away. You can paddle through the city of Richmond and feel like you're a million miles away. On the other end I like it because of the adrenaline rush when you're doing whitewater. Sometimes I talk about paddling being my therapy. On a hot summer day, after a hard day at work, there is nothing better than to get on the river for an hour or two of paddling. ≈

Paddling Tips & Rapids Ratings for the James River in Richmond

(Adapted from information provided by the Virginia Commission of Outdoor Recreation.)

Paddling Tips

- Tell someone where you are going and when you will be back.

- Know the river level at Westham Gauge; use increased caution as the river rises above 5 feet.

- Make sure everyone has a personal flotation device and helmet.

- If your boat capsizes in WHITEWATER, get away from it and attempt to stay on its upstream side. Once you have gotten clear of the boat, float through the rapids on your back with your feet up and pointed downstream to fend off rocks and other obstructions. (If you swamp in FLATWATER, hang on to the boat.)

- Be prepared for emergencies. Depending on the type of boat, carry a first aid kit, spare paddle, a proper and readily available rescue line, dry clothing, repair kit, bailer and a garbage bag.

- Respect the rights of non-paddlers taking part in other forms of river-oriented recreation.

- Never attempt to run low-water bridges or dams. Both can be extremely dangerous.

- Never paddle alone. Plan your trip for at least two people and preferably two or more boats. ≈

Rapids:
Difficulty Ratings

Sally Wetzler in challenging rapids.

- **CLASS I:** Occasional small rapids with low, regular waves not over one-foot high. Course easily determined. Rescue spots all along. Shallow.

- **CLASS II:** More frequent rapids. Eddies and whirlpools offer no trouble. Ledges not over three feet high with a direct uncomplicated chute. Course easily determined. Waves up to three feet high but avoidable. Water more than three feet deep.

- **CLASS III:** Long rapids, maneuvering required. Course not easily recognizable. Waves up to five feet high, mostly regular, avoidable; strong cross currents; a good rescue spot after each rapid.

- **CLASS IV:** Long rapids, intricate maneuvering. Course hard to determine, waves high (up to five feet), irregular, avoidable; or medium (up to three feet) and unavoidable; strong cross currents, eddies.

- **CLASS V:** Long continuous rapids, tortuous; requires frequent scouting. Extremely complex course. Waves large, irregular, unavoidable. Large-scale eddies and cross-currents. Rescue spots few and far off.

- **CLASS VI:** Long continuous rapids without let-up. Very tortuous, always scout. Waves high (about five feet), irregular, unavoidable; powerful cross- currents. Special equipment, limit of canoeability, involves risk of life. ≈

Top Three Paddling Tips from
Patrick Griffin of RVA Paddlesports

1
Don't stand in moving current.

2
Wear a PFD when the river level is above five feet.

3
Avoid lowhead dams, strainers (trees/debris), & pilings.

Swimming & Wading

The urban James River looks so inviting to swimmers and waders in so many places. But we have to remember that it's not a swimming pool; there are no lifeguards, no filtration systems, no diving boards, no smooth bottom, no lights, and no posted rules. Swimming and wading can be very enjoyable, but the key phrase is SAFETY FIRST.

Look at the PLACES section of this book and you'll find areas to safely wade and swim. And among those places, Tredegar Beach gets my nomination as the safest. It's sandy, shallow, calm, populated with all ages, and adjacent to the street in case there is an emergency. But there are plenty of other places — Belle Isle and Pony Pasture top the list — that are winners in the category of natural beauty and ambience.

It's important to be very aware of the following cautions.

1. Children should wear personal floatation devices at all times, and everyone should wear them when the river is higher than five feet at the Westham Gauge. (Google Westham Gauge and you'll find it on any of several websites.)

2. The river can rise quickly — as fast as a couple of feet in a couple of hours — because of rain west of Richmond. So pay attention to upstream rain, from Goochland all the way to Lynchburg.

3. Wear closed-toe shoes. The bottom of the river has a lot of natural danger such as rocks and limbs, and also manmade danger such as rebar, broken glass, and sharp metal.

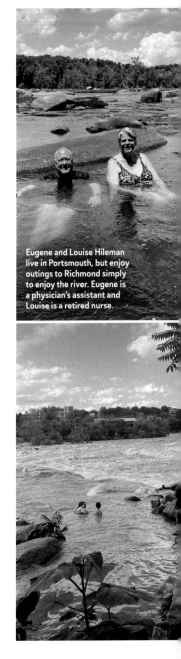

Eugene and Louise Hileman live in Portsmouth, but enjoy outings to Richmond simply to enjoy the river. Eugene is a physician's assistant and Louise is a retired nurse.

❹ Be careful when traversing rocks and boulders to get to swimming locations; they can be slippery.

❺ **NEVER** dive into the water or jump from high places.

❻ Be wary of the river's current. In waist-deep water even a moderate current can sweep

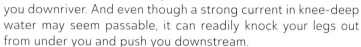

you downriver. And even though a strong current in knee-deep water may seem passable, it can readily knock your legs out from under you and push you downstream.

❼ If you do get caught in the current, drift downstream feet-first with your feet near the surface until you find a safe place to get out of the current.

❽ There is no need to worry about dangerous fish or animals; seemingly scary critters such as snapping turtles, longnose gar, flathead catfish, and various snakes haven't harmed anyone on the Richmond portion of the James River.

❾ Healthwise, the river is safe for swimming and wading EXCEPT for 48 hours or so after a torrential rain in Richmond. The city's storm water overflow system can back up into the wastewater system and empty some into the river. According to the website of the James River Association (**thejamesriver.org**), "James River Watch data shows that on average the river is generally safe for recreation, with 83% of all samples taken over the past five years meeting the state's safety standard. The other 17% of samples that showed high levels of bacteria were primarily found after significant rain events, which wash bacteria pollution into the river from surrounding land or from sewage systems." ≈

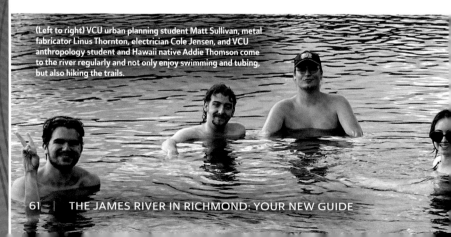

(Left to right) VCU urban planning student Matt Sullivan, metal fabricator Linus Thornton, electrician Cole Jensen, and VCU anthropology student and Hawaii native Addie Thomson come to the river regularly and not only enjoy swimming and tubing, but also hiking the trails.

Climbing

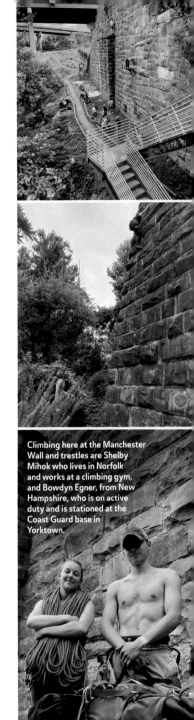

There are two climbing locations along the urban James: the Manchester Wall, located at the south end of the T. Tyler Potterfield Memorial Bridge, and the granite wall at the Belle Isle Quarry Pond.

The Manchester Wall, along with its accompanying three pillars, has the respect not only of local climbers, but is also known by climbers well beyond Richmond. To get to the Wall from the south side of the river, park in the small lot at the intersection of 7th and Semmes and follow the trail (a long walk). From the north side of the river access the Wall via the T. Tyler Potterfield Memorial Bridge.

There are more than 40 charted routes on the Wall and pillars, rated from 5.4 to 5.11a. Information and photos can be found on several websites (just Google) including the excellent local site peakexperiences.com.

This area's climbing opportunities were pioneered just over 40 years ago. Over the years the Wall has seen a variety of hardware installed, removed, and newly installed. Old bolts and anchors have been replaced with glue-in anchors that are regularly inspected. There are routes for both new and experienced climbers, and that offer rappelling, top-roping, and leading. And the trails leading to the Wall, as well as the landscaping of the immediate area, see continual improvements thanks in large part to organized volunteers.

A great way to gain an appreciation of the Wall and its keepers is to watch the video at this site: www.groundworksusa.org/story/manchester-wall/ And there are of course several good YouTube videos that feature actual climbing at the Wall.

Climbing here at the Manchester Wall and trestles are Shelby Mihok who lives in Norfolk and works at a climbing gym, and Bowdyn Egner, from New Hampshire, who is on active duty and is stationed at the Coast Guard base in Yorktown.

Rob Carter and Jamie McGrath, two of the persons who pioneered climbing on the Wall, wrote the following (slightly paraphrased here) — still relevant and important — just over 25 years ago.

"In 1981 four local climbers — Jamie McGrath, Les Newman, Rick Atkinson, and Ron Dawson — sauntered across Brown's Island in downtown Richmond to climb an imposing railroad pillar at the edge of the James River. Scrambling down a steep levy, and bushwhacking through briars and underbrush, the

climbers came to the second pillar, and the east-facing wall rising 60 feet above the river. The climb they had established on this pillar was tenuously protected by quarter-inch bolts and homemade hangers fashioned from angle iron. Peering out across the boulder waters, the group spotted for the first time a triangular bridge abutment set into the earth on the opposite bank of the river. In the years to follow, this massive bridge support, known as the Manchester Wall, would become the center of climbing activity in Richmond.

"From the Manchester Wall, a line of monoliths stretches across the entire width of the river. Only those pillars on the sides of the river are accessible, the majority of them rising from the currents of the river, teasing climbers with unseen routes. The pillars are remnants of the Richmond-Petersburg railroad bridge, a 19th century engineering marvel; and while they are manmade, the nearly vertical pylons offer climbers challenging face climbing.

Hair stylist Maria Papelino and violinist Sarah Agrios, photographed here at the Manchester Wall, began "serious" climbing two years ago. Their other James River Park activities include hiking, cycling, swimming and kayaking (beginners).

"The first known route on the Manchester Wall, The Proctologist, was put up by Les Newman, Jamie McGrath, Rick Atkinson, and Ron Dawson around 1981. This 5.9 route was protected by the same quarter-inch bolts and angle iron hangers that they had used on the north pillars. The bolts were driven only a half inch into the rock. Over the years

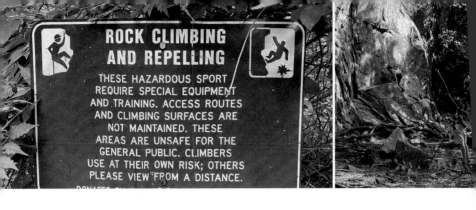

these bolts took many falls.

"From about 1986 to 1992 a handful of climbers visited the Wall on a regular basis, and it was during this time that most of the existing routes were established. The original group includes Jamie McGrath, Greg Elliott, Mossy Rowe, Keith Donovan, Barry McKenna, Rob Carter, Tyler Waybright, Mike Hutcheson, Keith Hall, Ed Wade and Noel Swinburn.

"By 1993 the Wall's quiet solitude was replaced by crowds; word of the Wall had spread beyond Richmond and sport climbing had arrived.

"Climbing the Wall and pillars is a unique experience. Clean granite blocks stacked one on top of another provide delicate face climbing. All of the vertical or nearly vertical routes consist of tiny edges, and the irregular, fragmented mortar joints connecting the blocks furnish larger holds and cracks for protection. Monodots scattered throughout the wall were originally drilled to enable the positioning of the massive granite stones. These provide single digit holds that regularly test finger strength. All of the routes can be top roped as well as led, and bouldering traverses provides great workouts. Any style of climbing is accepted at the Wall as long as it does not infringe upon the enjoyment and rights of other climbers or alter the appearance and integrity of the rock. Climbing is an inherently dangerous activity. Anyone climbing in the Manchester Wall area is responsible for his/her own safety."

Rob and Jamie's writings concluded with the following — still valid today: "Just a long rope length away from the Wall is the Legend Brewery. This microbrewery is a gathering place for climbers and other outdoor enthusiasts. On tap is a plentitude of fine brews."

The granite rock at the Belle Isle Quarry Pond is a much-used location for climbing/rappelling classes and camps for youth. There are 15-20 routes, some of which are bolted. Most of the routes are between 30 and 40 feet. Caution should be taken on the trail to get to the top anchors. There are very sketchy areas and a rappel is recommended to set them up.

I highly recommend the following YouTube video prior to climbing the Belle Isle Quarry Pond rock: W4F Rock Climbing Belle Isle Richmond VA. ≈

Jesse McCoy and 9-year-old son Harry enjoy April shad and striper fishing along the Floodwall.

Friends Sydney Owens (Virginia Tech student majoring in nutrition/exercise), Bella Richey (ODU majoring in business administration), and Katryn Combs (ODU, nursing) grew up in Richmond and enjoy the river's rocks and rapids.

Rowing

Go to Rocketts Landing most any dawn and you'll likely see shells being launched. Rowers enjoy that section of the river early in the day before the motor-boaters become active. There are three opportunities for rowers in Richmond. Adults become involved with the Virginia Boat Club and with Richmond Community Rowing that make use of the Rocketts Landing site as well as Robious Landing upstream. "The Virginia Boat Club offers members the opportunity to enjoy miles of scenic recreational and competitive rowing on the James River." The Club offers instruction, competition, and recreation for adults 18 and older. Detailed information can be found at vbc.godaddysites. com, on Facebook (Virginia Boat Club), and by e-mailing admin@ virginiaboatclub.org. Richmond Community Rowing embraces

its mission "to make rowing and other water sports available to the community regardless of background, ability, or experience." The organization offers adaptive programs, competitive programs, high school rowing, development camps, corporate rows, and veteran's rowing. For more info, go to richmondcommunityrowing.com. The third opportunity for rowers is River City Crew — a nonprofit organization for 8th—12th-graders. It operates out of Robious Landing Park and offers competitions and camps. For more information, go to rivercitycrew.org.

Fishing

The fishing question I get most often is this: "Where can I take my children to catch some fish on the James River in Richmond?" And it's followed by, "What lures and baits and methods work best?" The unfortunate answer is that although the river offers some really good fishing opportunities, there just aren't any opportunities for easy fishing with children. At least not easy fishing that's accompanied by catching. Most of the really productive fishing/catching requires hiking a long way and/or rock-hopping and/or wading and/or good casting skills and/or boating in moving water — thus not ideal for inexperienced children. Nevertheless, I'll offer three spots and methods that can usually result in your children catching fish.

Daniel and "F" (declined full names) enjoy fishing in the Dry Rocks area.

❶ Hike out onto the Dry Rocks area when the river level is below five feet and you'll see a lot of small channels and shallow pools. Select a pool that's at least a foot deep and that has water running into it. Any type of child's rod/reel will work here. At the end of the line tie a #8 hook, and a foot above the hook attach a 16th-ounce weight, and a foot above that attach any sort of float/bobber. Bait the hook with a worm or a grasshopper (or even a half-inch square of bacon). Toss it into the water and wait for the bobber to indicate a bite. There are little fish in those Dry Rocks pools and your child is guaranteed to get bites and hopefully even catch a few fish.

❷ Drive to the huge concrete wharf that you can enter via Wharf Street where Nicholson Street meets East Main. There is a huge parking area. Take something to sit on. Your child will need an adult-size rod and reel here. Make sure the line is at least 12-pound test. You'll need a #4 hook, a barrel swivel (any size), and a half-ounce egg sinker. Cut an 18-inch piece of line and put it aside for now. Now slide your main line through the egg sinker and then tie the swivel to the end of that line. Now tie the 18-inch piece of line to the swivel and then tie the #4 hook to the end of that line. Bait the hook with a dime-size piece of meaty bait: cut squid, chicken liver, cut fish, or even a glob of worms. Cast out as far as you can, sit back and relax and wait. When a fish bites, the rod will twitch. Wait for only 10 minutes, then reel in and cast again — preferably in another direction. You'll see other anglers fishing along this large dock area, and most are usually glad to offer advice and suggestions. And your child will enjoy watching as others reel in occasional fish.

3 Go to Pump House Park and find a spot to sit along the main canal. (A child's rod/reel will work fine here.) Tie on a rig just like the one for the large concrete wharf, but use a #8 hook and a quarter-ounce egg sinker. And for bait use a worm or grasshopper or cricket or even a dime-size piece of bacon. Cast it out and let it sink to the bottom and wait. In ten minutes cast in another direction. There are fish in the canal, and you'll eventually get bit!

For anglers who already have some experience, there is a fundamental fact about Richmond's James River: the 14th Street Bridge sits atop the Fall Line (the upstream reach of the ocean's tides) and is the dividing line for two totally different fisheries. Upstream consists

JC Gilmore-Bryan at the Kanawha Canal at Pump House Park.

of rocks, boulders, quickly moving water, and smallmouth bass. Downstream is slow-moving water and largemouth bass. Upstream also offers flathead catfish (some VERY large), channel catfish, and various "sunfish." Downstream offers channel catfish, blue catfish (some VERY large), crappie, white perch, springtime shad and stripers, and a sprinkling of other catchable fish.

Catching channel catfish on both sections can be successful using the same method: chicken liver (or some other stinky bait) on the bottom. Catching big flathead catfish (upstream section) is most successful by using a live fish (such as a small bluegill) for bait. Catching big blue cats (downstream) is most successful using live or cut eel or shad on the bottom. Of course success for catfish requires trying different locations and depths until you find them.

Much of the water upstream from the 14th Street Bridge is wadeable and/or rock-hopable, and the farther you can get from the shoreline and other persons the better. Between the 14th Street Bridge and Huguenot Flatwater there are many, many runs and pools and rapids that rarely see a fishing lure. Smallmouth bass are the prize fish here, and several methods can be successful — including simply drifting a live minnow through likely spots. Favorite lures for conventional tackle include grubs in earth colors, swimming minnow lures such as Rapala, topwater lures such as a Tiny Torpedo, and in-line spinners such as Mepps. Whatever lure you use, your best success will come when you fish "far and fine" (thin line and long casts). My favorite areas that offer great wading opportunities include Pony Pasture, the 42nd Street Entrance, and beneath the south side of the Boulevard Bridge (wade upstream).

Downstream from the 14th Street Bridge, largemouth bass are the prize fish in this section of the river, but they can be hard to find without a boat — mostly because there isn't a lot of shoreline accessibility. There are a zillion lures and methods that will catch the river's largemouth bass, but if I had to narrow it to three, I'd go with the following. One would be any type of dark color 5-inch Senko, fished wacky-style (hook through

▲ PICTURED ABOVE: Justen Layne with 4-pound largemouth from the tidal James.

▼ PICTURED BELOW: Former Chicagoan David McFadden fishes all year along the shoreline immediately upstream from Ancarrow's Landing. Here he holds an April shad that he retrieved from his cooler for this photo. The rest of the year he fishes mostly for catfish using cut bait.

70

the middle) without a weight and cast to any sort of cover (shorelines, rocks, pilings, stumps, etc.). A second would be a blue/chrome quarter-ounce Rat-L-Trap used as a "search bait" in all types of water. And a third would be a 200-Series Bandit crankbait in some sort of gray color: cast it anywhere to dive up to eight feet deep.

During the month of April American Shad, Hickory Shad, and Stripers head upstream to spawn and are halted when they reach the beginning of the river's rapids — beneath the 14th Street Bridge. That part of the river — the half mile or so beneath and downstream from the 14th Street Bridge — becomes packed with fish and with anglers who fish from boats and from the south shore.

Shad and Stripers are the prizes and the formulas for catching them are straightforward. The best shad lures are small gold and silver shiny spoons (sometimes one color works better than the other) and small white or chartreuse (eighth- and sixteenth-ounce) hair jigs. Very light line is needed to cast these small lures, and many anglers add a quarter-ounce weight a foot or so above the lure to get extra distance. Just cast them out and reel them in. Try different speeds for the retrieve so the lure can search various depths.

Stripers will hit a variety of big topwater lures that "spit," "walk," and "buzz." They will also hit shiny lipless crankbaits such as a blue/chrome Rat-L-Trap and white jigs with curly plastic trailers. Bait anglers catch stripers using cut shad and cut eel.

White perch are among the "supporting cast" of April's smorgasbord, and they can be caught on small curly-tail jigs and small shiny lures such as spoons and in-line spinners such as Mepps. And they'll hit live worms as well as a variety of cut bait. Use small hooks.

More and more fly-fishing anglers are seen on the river: in April catching shad using weighted lines and bright streamers (almost always from boats), and wading upstream using topwaters and wooly buggers for smallmouths and sunfish. Of course every fly angler has favorite patterns and my experience confirms that they are always willing to share their expertise. The upstream river is a fly angler's heaven: runs and riffles and pools and boulders and nothing very deep. AND, once out in the river, there are no trees to hinder your casts.

December through February are tough months for catching

Vintage John Bryan

much of anything on the upstream James. Success comes with lures/baits that move very slowly. Slow-drifting minnows through deep pools is one method that sometimes works. The downstream river continues to produce fish year-round, but slow and deep presentations work best. Wintertime artificial lures for bass include jigs with plastic trailers, deep crankbaits, and jigging spoons. Catfish can be caught year-round on cut bait. ≈

Alex McCrickard on Fishing

Alex McCrickard, Aquatic Education Coordinator for Virginia's Department of Wildlife Resources, has a lot of expertise regarding fishing — especially fly-fishing — on the urban James River. **He offers three suggestions.**

1. Although the river is large, fish it like it's small. Become familiar with a small part of the river and fish its braids and pockets.

2. Match the hatch. Fish lures and flies that look similar to the prevailing underwater and topwater life that is currently available: nymphs, crayfish, minnows, grasshoppers, mayflies, damselflies, etc.

3. A great place to start is the Pony Pasture area; there are lots of productive and relatively untouched areas that can be reached by wading and rock-hopping out into the river.

Discover the River with Mike Ostrander

The website is discoverthejames.com and the guide is long-time river veteran Mike Ostrander. Pictured here downstream from Richmond at Osborne Landing, Mike operates what he calls an "eco-based business" that includes outings on the Richmond portion of the river. Mike offers outings that focus on bald eagles, osprey, herons, sturgeon, photography, history, as well as custom-arranged tours.

Photography

The work of professional photographer Richard Hayes, co-founder of RVAHUB, includes activities along the James River in Richmond, including here at the Richmond International Dragon Boat Festival.

More than 20 years ago, Ralph White wrote a very comprehensive "Photographers' and Painters' Guide to the James River Park System" and introduced it with this: "The rugged rocks, crashing waters, historic ruins and wooded landscape of the Fall Line of the James River lend themselves to dramatic pictures. There is also abundant wildlife (including rare and endangered species) and people doing exciting things — like rock climbing, whitewater boating and mountain biking. It is a place to capture dramatic vistas, tiny vignettes of nature and moments of human adventure. The special beauty is that it is all relatively close and easy to access."

The James River in Richmond offers a photographer's smorgasbord of flora and fauna, songbirds and raptors, rippling rapids and quiet pools, artifacts and ruins, skylines and tree lines, cityscapes and waterscapes, bridges and boulders, and every slice of humanity. Where best to take pictures? Depends. Find plenty of revelers of all cultures and ages at river sites such as Pony Pasture and Belle Isle or at riverside festivals and events on Brown's Island and along the Canal Walk. Look for water adventurers at Hollywood Rapids and Pipeline Rapids, and waterside anglers at Ancarrow's Landing and Rocketts Landing Wharf.

Want photos of elusive mammals such as river otters? Make daybreak visits to Texas Beach or Belle Isle. Birders take their cameras to the heights: the Floodwall Walk and the pedestrian and vehicle bridges. Want flowers and trees? The Wetlands area and the Reedy Creek area offer flowery meadows and varietal woodlands.

Interested in photographing history? It's everywhere: old bridge supports, fish trap drill holes in the river's boulders, metal and stone skeletons of commercial enterprises, carved granite blocks that wall the

nation's first canals, and on and on.

Best all-around places to take photos? I'll narrow it to two: the Pipeline (accessible only to the nimble-footed) and the T. Tyler Potterfield Memorial Bridge (accessible to everyone). The T-Pott offers photo-worthy views of almost everything mentioned above, while the Pipeline offers seemingly secret, confidential, undiscovered views of the glory of nature and the underbelly of city-building. (Visit them and you'll see for yourself.)

Ralph White's guide suggests dozens of examples of specific subject matter, including the following: architectural features such as the concentric semicircles of the bridge supports under the Manchester Bridge, Memorial Day crowds lying on the rocks at Pony Pasture, splotchy white and green bark patterns of winter Sycamore trees, late-fall sunrise mist on the river at Pony Pasture, city skyline with flashing glass windows at sunrise or sunset (from the western end of the Floodwall), and Great Blue Herons during courtship (spring along the Pipeline). ≈

Bill Draper on Photography

Bill Draper, a prolific photographer of the urban James, offers five suggestions.

1. Early morning is the golden hour — the time to see wildlife.

2. The Lee Bridge provides a great overlook of the river.

3. A favorite "small" place is the Pipeline in the spring because of the abundance of Great Blue Herons.

4. The bike lane of the Manchester Bridge offers prime photo opportunities.

5. The southside Floodwall provides views of feeding Ospreys and Eagles that chase them.

74

History

The James River's Fall Line — the place where its hundreds of miles of downhill currents and rapids end and meet the calm water that rises up and down each day with the 125-mile reach of the ocean's tides — is located precisely beneath today's 14th Street Bridge in Richmond. The Fall Line has, perhaps more than anything else, been the most influential element in the history of Richmond.

Native Americans focused on the Fall Line's annual congregations of anadromous fish being hindered in their upstream spawning runs, and the birds and mammals that populated the area, and the multi-branched food chain — both flora and fauna — that prospered from the diverse habitat of the Fall Line.

America's first Europeans, in a boat captained by Christopher Newport, were halted by the Fall Line on their upriver exploration of the new continent. Claiming the newly visited land for England, they placed a wooden cross at the site of today's 14th Street Bridge.

With settlement and population growth came agriculture, industry and trade. Richmond's location allowed ocean-going vessels to arrive on one side of the Fall Line while water power was harnessed to energize mills and factories on the other side. At one point Richmond was the nation's largest city — eventually surpassed by New York City. During the 1860s Richmond river traffic had increased to 4,000 vessels per year. And during Richmond's phenomenal growth from 1830 until the Civil War, the city was, according to Brenton S. Halsey's book, *Riverfront Renaissance*, "on a per capita basis, perhaps the wealthiest in the world." Of course the purchase and sale and labor of enslaved persons — Richmond's Fall Line location was ideal for slave trade — was a major factor in the city's growth and prosperity.

Richmond's national and industrial prominence and robustness declined after the Civil War, and the importance of the river's Fall Line dwindled. But with the 1960s ("the dawning of the age of Aquarius") there began a vision of a future new importance for the Fall Line: beauty, nature and recreation. At first there were few voices in this both metaphorical and literal wilderness, but they were gradually joined by power-brokers, decision-makers, and persons of influence. The James River eventually became Richmond's best amenity — not for industry and trade, but for sheer enjoyment.

In 2012, after careful examination of 50 candidate cities, *Outside Magazine* declared Richmond to be the nation's best river city. And in 2019 the James River received the prestigious Thiess International Riverprize that "champions integrated river basin management for the restoration, protection and sustainable management of the world's rivers...by facilitating leadership, celebration and collaboration."

It would take many volumes to chronicle the history of the James River in Richmond. This guidebook offers suggestions for those who want to learn about the history.

1 Explore the paths and walkways along both sides of the river and read the abundant signage. The 22 bronze medallions along the Canal Walk are a great place to start. Each presents an element of history: the nation's first electric trolley, the Powhatan Chiefdom, Belle Isle, and on and on.

2 Read books: Ralph Hambrick's *Transforming the James River in Richmond*, especially Chapter 11, "Showcase for History;" Brenton S. Halsey's *Riverfront Renaissance*, especially the first 11 pages; *The Falls of the James Atlas* by W.E. Trout III, James Moore, III, and George D. Rawls, "the most comprehensive book there is on

Tobacco Row

Boxing tobacco leaves, ca. 1900

the historical artifacts in and alongside Richmond's urban James River;" David D. Ryan's marvelous chronicle of the river's Richmond history in his *The Falls of the James*; and of course Bob Deans' *The River Where American Began*. (For more, see the BOOKS section of this guidebook.)

③ Take a Riverfront Canal Cruise, "40-minute historically narrated boat tours of the James River and Kanawha Canal along downtown Richmond's Historic Canal Walk."

④ Take Richmond History Tours presented by the Valentine Museum (thevalentine.org).

⑤ Do Internet research about your own discoveries along the river. There are artifacts of history everywhere.

⑥ Notice the nuggets of history sprinkled throughout this guidebook.

The history of the James River in Richmond abounds along its shorelines and within its currents. We can be its devotees and keepers. History can help us understand ourselves and our community. And it can provide knowledge that fosters empathy and even kindness.

A Walk on the Slave Trail

On a perfect-weather Sunday afternoon I'm walking the riverside portion of the Slave Trail: from Ancarrow's Landing to the top of the Floodwall. The Slave Trail is the path that enslaved persons — children and adults, mostly in shackles — walked to downtown Richmond after being unloaded from transport boats, and then in later years from downtown Richmond to boats waiting to take them to the deep south.

Today the granite-block shoreline where the boats docked those many years ago is populated by happy families fishing and lounging and picnicking and snoozing. The scene is sprinkled with occasional bikers and hikers. I watch a dark-skin, blue-dressed little girl climb a small tree near her picnic-blanketed family.

Carefully considered signage informs the Slave Trail — signage that confirms the greatest shame of our city and our river. Richmond was the country's slave trade capital. The Trail's signage details numbers and events and horrors, and aligns the fortunes of slavery to the "progress" of Richmond.

I complete the Slave Trail's brief path along the former docking wall as it enters thick woods. At the entrance to the woods, just ten feet from an especially disturbing sign, relaxes a Black family — mother, father, grandmother, three children. Might they be descendants of enslaved persons who walked here back then?

"... the poor wretches being travel-worn and half starved, and having large sores caused by their loads and the blows and cuts they received ... one woman still carrying the infant that had died in her arms of starvation."

The Trail is nicely mulched as it snuggles into the greenery of the woods. A helmeted and suited biker whizzes toward me and smiles "Thank you" as I step aside to let him pass. Others whom I will encounter on this Trail — bikers and walkers — will exhibit similar friendliness.

A short ways into the woods I encounter a handsomely carpentered footbridge that crosses a narrow runoff ravine. Then a bit farther is another, and at the bottom of this ravine is a concrete structure atop which a mother and son hold fishing rods. Adjacent to the Trail at this point — just 50 feet or so out of the woods — is roadside parking for a dozen or so cars.

Prior to a third footbridge — the path still running through thick woods — is a pair of Day-lilies. One has a broken stalk and hugs the ground; the other rises high — perhaps 3 feet — atop a sturdy stalk.

"... a major port in the massive downriver slave trade, making Richmond the largest source of enslaved blacks on the east coast of America from 1830 to 1860."

Richmond
SLAVE TRAIL

HISTORIC SLAVE TRAIL

MECHANICS OF SLAVERY

78

Soon the path narrows and compresses into a crawl tunnel beneath a half-fallen tree and its accompanying foliage and vines — the only spot on the entire Trail that is the least bit uncomfortable or constricting. There was of course an absence of any sort of comfort on this Trail during the years of slave trade.

The Trail parallels the river, and as I near the I-95 bridge I start to see glimpses of downtown Richmond. I hear cars and trucks and motorcycles as they zoom the bridge.

The Trail leaves the woods at the I-95 Bridge. On both sides of the adjacent road there is under-bridge parking for dozens of cars. I walk beneath the bridge toward the river and I see a handful of anglers — adults with children. Near a parked van is a food table around which a dozen persons gather.

Just west of the bridge is the Floodwall gate through which I walk on the Trail as it follows the spine of the Floodwall hill. The Trail climbs up and up and then offers a fork downslope toward the river to join the paved Floodwalk Walk. But I continue upward to the top of the hill where this path deadends at another sign about the Trail, a sign entitled, "Richmond's Burgeoning Trade" — the "trade" of course being human beings.

Next to the sign is a modest little bench upon which I sit and view today's downtown Richmond and contemplate the historic context.

"Several dozen slave auction houses operated in Shockoe Bottom, supporting the lucrative sugar and cotton plantations in the deep south."

The downhill fork, which I didn't take, is the route of the remainder of the Slave

Trail: upstream to the 14th Street Bridge and then across the river, through Shockoe Bottom, and then uphill to the site where existed the notorious Lumpkin's Jail — one of several where enslaved persons were housed and tortured and bought and sold. I don't walk that part of the Trail today; I've walked and driven it many times before.

My challenge now is to determine a fresh poignancy for this Slave Trail — something that hasn't been already well cliché'd. My walk today is comfortable and relaxed; that of enslaved persons wasn't. The Trail today is well-manicured, easy on the feet, and without disturbance; the Trail of enslaved persons was none of those. My brain is relaxed and welcoming to external stimulation; enslaved persons were certainly tormented with fright, uncertainty, and anguish. But each of these observations is obvious, easily determined, and so well documented and dramatized that the shock value has lost much of its impact.

"During the years of Trans-Atlantic trade of enslaved Africans to North America, white Virginians purchased roughly 114,000 from Atlantic slaving brigs."

There are a few things that I've encountered in person that are so remarkable, so unimaginable, so stunning, that they have caused me to simply stop and think. To think deeply. The Grand Canyon and the Viet Nam Memorial are that way. No matter how much you read, no matter how many photos and films you see, no matter how many persons tell you about their experiences there, there's just no way to understand unless you experience it in person.

My thought is that the Slave Trail is not like that. The pathway is unremarkable. There are no alligator-infested swamps, no narrow fall-

off ledges, no thickets of briars. It's simply a nicely manicured path through the woods followed by well-attended pavement. It has zero resemblance to the journey that enslaved persons took. The signage is the only way that most Trail visitors know what happened here.

Will I have some sort of epiphany here? Will I experience a profundity? Will today's walk on the Slave Trail transform me? Enlighten me?

"Bound beneath the ship's deck, this cargo of men, women, and children were routinely deprived of adequate food and water and subjected to savage treatment as the slave ships hurled and lurched toward to an unknown fate."

On the ground I see and pick up something that I recognize: a six-inch junebug-colored Senko — a fishing lure the size and shape of a ballpoint pen. Gary Yamamoto conceived the lure years ago when he dropped his pen into the water and observed its unique wobble as it sunk. I've caught lots of bass from this river on Senkos.

I look out on the river and see an angler moving slowly in a small boat. Nearby are two paddleboards and a kayak going in the opposite direction. And paralleling the river on the far shore a train passes.

I walk the home stretch of the Trail back where I began, and I again see the blue-skirted girl — now helping her red-skirted little sister climb the same tree.

But this is where *"enslaved Africans were 'sold down the river' to plantation owners ready to pay premium prices that allowed traders to amass huge fortunes. Receipts from slave sales in 1857 approached $3.5 million dollars (equal to more than $100 million today)."*

And as I approach my car, and the container of ice water that waits there, I spot a small Ladybug on my shirt sleeve. As I remove and release it, I consider its near-global symbolism: the appearance of a Ladybug means that wishes and dreams are coming to fruition. ≈

Canals along the Urban James

During the 19th Century Richmond's main commerce to the western part of the state was via the river and Kanawha Canal. The primary goods that traveled on the canal were lumber, coal, tobacco, corn, wheat, stone and iron ore. But by the turn of the century railroads had taken over.

As America was being settled, rivers provided the easiest access west. Gradually the idea of building canals to connect rivers on both sides of mountains became dominant. This idea was of course dependent on first making the rivers navigable. This included making sluices (channels through shallow areas of the river), diversion dams (to direct water in a certain direction), and riverside canals to bypass difficult areas of the river.

In 1765 the Virginia General Assembly first authorized the building of a canal to bypass the Falls of the James — approximately seven miles from Westham to Richmond. For the next 100 years the Kanawha Canal was an ongoing project along much of the length of the James.

The seven-mile falls section of the Kanawha Canal was completed in 1795. Virtually all of the work was done by hand. They used hand tools, wagons, and dangerous black powder. Blasting holes were drilled by hand into the rocks.

Always a concern was to build the canal such that it would stay full of water. Feeder dams and feeder channels often had to be built.

Also the canal had to have enough bank to separate it from the river's floods. Plus, it had to have a parallel ditch to carry rainwater and a parallel towpath for the livestock that towed the boats.

Finally, there was the formidable challenge of making the canal hold water. Even lining the canal with clay often didn't stop leaks. Animals were also sources of holes for leaks.

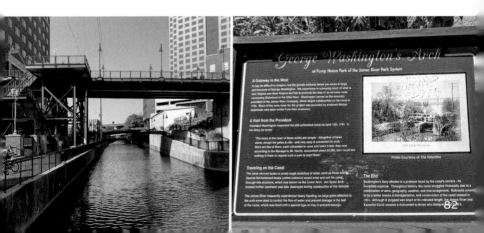

A lot of the work on the early sections of the canal — especially around the Falls of the James — was done by rented slaves. Because of the difficult conditions and modest wages, white workers could be sources of complaints.

By 1808 the James River Company — which had financed the canal with much risk, many hardships, and much more expense than had been anticipated — was making a good profit. The James River Company had "cleared" the river all the way to Buchanan, and goods could be floated — precariously — all the way to Richmond. Politics, troubles, and complaints eventually resulted in the James River Company's transfer to state ownership in 1820.

The transfer did not result in much improvement, and in 1832 a new private company was authorized: the James River and Kanawha Company. In spite of expenses, floods, continual problems, and the growing reliability of railroads, sections of the Kanawha Canal were built and improved all along the river from Richmond to Buchanan — with the visionary goal of connecting to the Ohio River. As the Civil War approached, the James River and Kanawha Company had reached its most active and prosperous time.

The War not only left the canal without maintenance, but it was also intentionally damaged along much of its length. By 1870 most sources of private and federal funds for the canal were gone.

The earliest boats used by both Indians and settlers were dugout canoes. They were followed by the bateaux which could hold much more. The canoes were approximately 50 feet long, and a bateau was slightly shorter but more than twice as wide. The bateaux were poled both downstream and back upstream, and were the largest boats able to navigate the rapids.

Next, with completion of more sections of the canal, came freight barges: approximately 90 feet long and 14 feet wide. They were pulled by mules.

For about 15 years there were also a few packet boats — 80 feet long and 11 feet wide — which were designed to carry people. The packet boat's limited space was continually convertible and had sections designated as dressing areas, dining areas, sleeping areas, kitchen, and bar. Travel on a packet boat could be a charming, slow, social experience. But everyone agreed that the cramped quarters made sleeping on a packet boat very unpleasant.

In 1880 all property of the James River and Kanawha Company was transferred to the Richmond and Allegheny Railroad, and tracks were soon laid along the towpath, thus ending all practical use of the canal.

Reynolds Metals Company preserved the stone locks at 12th and Byrd Streets and published a brochure about "The James River and Kanawha Canal." The brochure concludes with a section entitled, "The Canal Today":

"The Tidewater Connection locks of the James River and Kanawha Canal have been preserved by the Reynolds Metals Company as part of the design of its Reynolds Wrap Distribution Center located at 12th and Byrd Streets in Richmond, Virginia.

"The double locks, Nos. 4 and 5 of the Tidewater Connection, are magnificent examples of the stonemason's art. Each lock is 100 feet long by 15 feet wide. The lock gates, constructed of wood, rotted through toward the end of the 19th Century.

"The 13th Street bridge, with its two arches, was built in 1860 by Richard B. Haxall and Lewis D. Crenshaw, proprietors of the nearby Haxall-Crenshaw Flour Mill. Their initials and the date of completion can be clearly seen inscribed on the key stone of the bridge spanning the canal.

"Many other works of the James River and Kanawha Canal are still present in Richmond today; including the Canal from Bosher's Dam west of the city to Gamble's Hill below 5th Street; the locks at the Pump House at Byrd Park, the Richmond Dock east of 17th Street and the Great Ship Lock at Dock and 26th Streets. These works are inscribed on the prestigious National Register of Historic Places and in the Virginia Landmarks Register." ≈

14th Street Bridge aka Mayo's Bridge

In 1607 Christopher Newport planted a cross at the location of today's 14th Street Bridge, but it was 181 years later that the first bridge was built over Richmond's James River. On October 26, 1788, John Mayo completed the first bridge to the city that his grandfather, William Mayo, had laid out in 1737.

It was a bad bridge — just a series of log rafts affixed to rocks with metal spikes. The breaking up of the first winter's ice completely destroyed it. Mayo quickly replaced the bridge — this time higher above the water and making use of more timber and loose granite — and he was back in business collecting tolls by the early fall.

What did the bridge connect? On the northern side of the river was Richmond proper, a busy business district with access to all the commerce of the incoming and outgoing ships and new canal system. On the south side was Manchester — also called Dogtown — which contained the other end of the financial spectrum: common workers and freed slaves. There were constant tensions between the inhabitants of the two sides, and the bridge's tolls added significantly to the ill will. A pedestrian paid a nickel, six cents if with a horse.

Throughout the 1880s natural phenomena including ice, but mostly floods, closed and destroyed the bridge over and over, causing it to be rapidly rebuilt over and over. Once Mayo's Bridge was destroyed purposefully — at the end of the Civil War when Confederate troops were evacuating Richmond and burned the bridge behind them. It was of course rebuilt within a few months.

Floods and ice continued to damage and destroy the bridge, and

in 1871 a new bridge was built out of iron. The new toll structure included a 15-cent fee for horse and buggy and continued to be 5 cents for a single person. The iron construction was not much better than wood in withstanding high water and ice, and in 1877 the bridge was again washed away by flood and again rapidly rebuilt. For 25 more years floods and ice and even snow continued regular destruction of the bridge.

Vintage Trevor Piersol beneath 14th Street Bridge.

Finally, in 1913, a new material — concrete — was used to build a new Mayo's Bridge. It was styled after the Pont Neuf bridge in Paris. This new bridge marked the passage from private to public hands. The city-owned, concrete Mayo's Bridge proved to be a formidable structure. It has thus far withstood everything with which nature has confronted it — including a handful of floods which covered the bridge entirely.

Today Mayo's Bridge — the 14th Street Bridge — connects Richmond's downtown high-rise business area with a newly blossoming Hull Street area that includes construction of more and more upscale apartment buildings.

Citizens from all parts of town commingle on and below the 14th Street Bridge every spring — citizens who like to fish. Every spring fishers congregate for the springtime arrival of stripers, shad, herring, white perch and other species there where the Atlantic Ocean's tidal waters meet the upstream rapids — the river's Fall Line. ≈

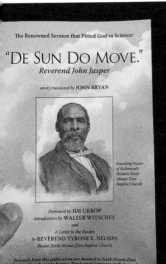

The Renowned Sermon that Pitted God vs Science:

"DE SUN DO MOVE."
Reverend John Jasper

newly translated by JOHN BRYAN

Founding Pastor of Richmond's Historic Sixth Mount Zion Baptist Church

Foreword by JIM UKROP
Introduction by WALTER WITSCHEY
and
A Letter to the Reader
by REVEREND TYRONE E. NELSON
Pastor, Sixth Mount Zion Baptist Church

Proceeds from this publication are donated to Sixth Mount Zion Baptist Church and to Baptist Theological Seminary at Richmond.

JOHN JASPER

On September 3, 1867 Reverend John Jasper, who had been born into slavery 55 years earlier, established Richmond's Sixth Mount Zion Baptist Church in a shanty on Brown's Island. By the time he first presented his hallmark sermon, entitled "De Sun Do Move," Jasper had already become a widely admired preacher. He went on to present the sermon 273 times in more than 250 venues, and newspapers as far away as Boston encouraged readers to travel to Richmond to hear Jasper preach. The theme of the sermon — God vs Science — can be especially relevant when experiencing the natural wonders of Richmond's James River. In 2008 I published a little booklet that contains the sermon; copies are available from Sixth Mount Zion Baptist Church.

Timeline Glimpses

1600s AND BEFORE
Algonquian Indians harvested eight- and nine-foot sturgeon from the river.

1607
After landing at Jamestown a week earlier, Christopher Newport arrived at the site of today's 14th Street Bridge.

1737
Earliest industry on the James was begun by William Byrd II who gave Richmond its name because the river bends here as it does at Richmond upon Thames.

1771
The Great Flood crested around 40 feet.

1780
Virginia's capital was moved from Williamsburg to Richmond because of the James River.

1785
James River Company incorporated to build the nation's first canal system.

1800
Hollywood Paper Mill was established along the north bank, and became a hydroelectric plant from 1940-1972.

1830
The first packet boats took passengers on ten-day trips from Richmond to Lynchburg using the James River and Kanawha Canal.

1836
Tredegar Iron Works — the foundry for the Confederacy — opened on the north bank of the James River.

1844 — 54
Canal use was at its peak, with 200 boats of various sizes.

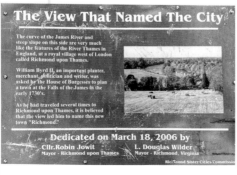

The View That Named The City

The curve of the James River and steep slope on this side are very much like the features of the River Thames in England, at a royal village west of London called Richmond upon Thames.

William Byrd II, an important planter, merchant, politician and writer, was asked by the House of Burgesses to plan a town at the Falls of the James in the early 1730's.

As he had traveled several times to Richmond upon Thames, it is believed that the view led him to name this new town "Richmond."

Dedicated on March 18, 2006 by
Cllr.Robin Jowit   L. Douglas Wilder
Mayor - Richmond upon Thames   Mayor - Richmond, Virginia

Richmond Sister Cities Commission

1862
Union prisoners-of-war were held on Belle Isle.

1958
Primary treatment was established for waste water entering the river.

1970
James River Park was dedicated.

1972
Hurricane Agnes, with a still-record crest of 36.5 feet, caused legislation and funding that ultimately spawned the Floodwall.

1994
The Richmond Floodwall Protection System was dedicated.

Vintage Thomas Bryan

1990s
New projects were completed, including the fish passage at Williams Dam, the Combined Sewer Overflow project that carries overflow closer to the sewage plant and out of the James River Park, the Bosher's Dam fishway ladder that allows migrating fish passage through Richmond, and the renovation of the Kanawha and Haxall Canals.

1999
The Canal Walk was dedicated.

2009
James River Park was placed in a conservation easement, thereby disallowing future commercial development.

2012
The Richmond Riverfront Plan was adopted.

2019
The James River received the prestigious Thiess International Riverprize, the world's foremost award in river basin management, and is among two dozen annual winners since 1999 such as the Rhine, Thames, Danube, and Mekong.

2020
James River Park became the most visited attraction in Richmond, with more than two million visits annually.

Nature

R ichmond's James River has an abundance of life in and around it. Cleaner water and protected lands have created a natural smorgasbord of flora and fauna. There are deer, beaver, river otters, muskrats, mink, foxes, etc. The urban river now has one of the nation's great concentrations of bald eagles. In the spring at the 14ᵗʰ Street Bridge the river teams with shad and striped bass. Wildflowers blossom most of the year (David Ryan's book, *The Falls of the James*, lists 471 species compiled by Newton Ancarrow), and the river is bordered by a forest of Blackgum, Sweetgum, Sycamore, Beech, Oaks, and many others. An occasional bear cub even winds up on the urban James after having followed the river corridor from its upstream nativity.

The urban James is rich with varieties of mammals, birds, mollusks, flowers, trees, wildflowers, plants, amphibians, fish, and rocks. And there are now mobile phone apps to assist with identification — especially with flowers, trees, and plants.

Where do you begin? That's easy: the website of Friends of James River Park: jamesriverpark. org. Under the EDUCATE tab, click the Science in the Park listing and you'll find lists of species found along the river: mammals, birds, butterflies, arthropods, plants, etc. There is information regarding geology and water. And there is even a Teacher Resources section along with Lesson Plans.

Vintage Susannah Piersol

Birding is popular along the urban James; over 100 species are regularly seen, and many others are spotted from time to time. Richmond is a natural flyway for migratory birds. Jerry Uhlman's 2014 book, *A Birder's Guide to Metropolitan Richmond*, is a good resource. And of course the Richmond Audubon Society provides wonderful outings.

Mammals are difficult to spot, and the best opportunities are at daybreak. But you can look for mammal tracks throughout the day. Trees, plants, and wildflowers are easily found and identified, and it can be enjoyable to identify leaves, fruits, and nuts in the fall. One caution is that poison ivy is abundant along the river and its wooded trails. Once you know what it looks like, it's easy to spot.

The backwaters, side channels, and sandbars of the river offer interesting natural discoveries: varieties of mollusks, frogs and tadpoles and minnows, water plants, and one of the most interesting ecosystems: rock potholes. Round potholes in rocks and boulders, sometimes a few feet deep, originate when pebbles get caught in a crack or fissure. The river's current then swirls them around and around as they slowly abrade the rock and form larger and larger

circular holes. This of course takes many, many years. The resulting mini-ecosystem can include a variety of plant and animal life.

James River Park, right in the middle of a 1.4 Million metropolitan area, is a natural wonderland. It's where the wild things are. Look anywhere, examine closely, and take photographs for later research.

Visitors from California — Kenney Reeves who does post production for reality television, and Alex Dell'Amico who works in real estate — have discovered Richmond's urban James River and have decided that they would love to have their wedding (planned for 2023) right here.

Bailey F**king Jones (legal name, left), traveled from Joshua Tree, California for VA Pridefest on Brown's Island that included a performance by Richmonder Cassidy Snider and her band, The Wranglers.

Snorkeling in the City

(Written by Ralph White and first published by the James River Park System)

Oriental Freshwater Clam — These clams are small (1/4 to 1 1/4 inches), round and often seen as piles of shells. Recently eaten ones may be found on top of rocks, put there by muskrats. Look for old ones distributed by water along the shoreline at the ends of islands and in the sand behind rocks.

These clams were first seen in the James River in the early 1970s, clogging up cooling pipes at an electric power plant near Hopewell. They were probably brought over in ballast water used to weigh down ships. No one knows what their impact on the environment will be, except that they filter the water in order to feed and have become very common. Small ones are eaten by Redbreast Sunfish and Bull Chubs.

Dig your hands into sand bars and fine gravel to find live ones. Watch them underwater as they dig back down by sticking their soft bodies out of their shells-sometimes they'll do this while you hold them between your fingers under water.

American Freshwater Mussel — The mussels are medium to large in size (one to five inches across) with a thin shell and have a slick, shiny lining. The flesh was once eaten by Native Americans, but is not safe to eat in the city areas now because they concentrate pollutants in their bodies by filter feeding. Some mussels from the Mississippi River are shipped to Japan where tiny bits of flesh and shell are added to Japanese oysters to stimulate pearl growth!

Feel the smooth, lustrous inside called "Mother of Pearl." It is the substance that pearls are made of and was once used to make buttons. Look for live mussels sticking up like a wedge in gravel bars where the water is a foot or less deep and moving quickly.

"Bowl-of-Sand Nests" — Look in calm water near the shore or behind boulders for these six-to-nine-inch-wide sunfish nests. Males guard the nests in June and July. With patient waiting you can see the male flair his fins and show his colors. This attracts nearby females and chases away any other fish that may try to eat the tiny eggs. Gently drop a tiny pebble or snail onto the nest and he'll quickly remove it by biting it and spitting it out away from the nest.

"Table-Top-of-Walnut-Sized Rocks Nest" — Look in moving water for these two-to-three-feet-wide Bull Chub nests. The male guards the nests but not very well. Watch other fish come up to the nest to lay their eggs or to eat someone else's!

Snails — There are at least a half-dozen kinds of aquatic snails in Richmond. Each has its own special water conditions, but many can be found near one another, often on the upstream and downstream sides of the same rock!

Long Spiral-shelled Snails — "River Snails" are the most common kind and have many ridges around the shell. A smooth-surfaced, thinner-shelled kind is a rare find.

Short Spiral-shelled Snails — "Pond Snails" are small and smooth with rounded edges. Another small, smooth kind has one wide, flat ridge around the edge. "Little Pond Snails" are tiny, thin, smooth and cone-shaped. Org Snails look like a coil of rope and are also rare.

Aquatic Insects — These bottom dwellers hatch and live underwater for most of their lives — six months to two years. They come out of the water, shed their skins, and become winged adults that breathe air. These live only a few days or weeks — long enough to mate and lay eggs in the water. At night the small water-dwelling nymphs and larvae feed on algae (and on each other) on top of submerged rocks. During the day they hide from fish under rocks. (That's why fish feed best at dawn and dusk!)

Nymphs live underwater and include the Mayfly nymph (three tails, legs in close), Stonefly nymph (two tails, legs held out), Damselfly nymph (three tails, legs held out), Dragonfly nymph (plump body), Caddisfly larva (green), and Hellgrammites (sharp pinchers and many legs).

In the air are the adult Mayfly (body arched with three tails), adult Stonefly (wings folded on back), adult Damselfly (wings held up over back — eat mosquitoes, do not sting), adult Dragonfly (large, wings to sides, do not sting, eat mosquitoes), adult Caddisfly (long antennae, moth-like wings), and adult Dobsonfly (large mouth parts, wings flat on back).

Vintage Thomas Bryan

Hold the Mayfly, Stonefly and Damselfly nymphs in your palm full of water. Watch them vibrate their "tails" and/or side flaps in the still water to get more oxygen. These are actually gills.

Cup some water in your hand with a Dragonfly nymph and watch it walk. Put one in a swim mask full of water and it can also move forward quickly by pumping water out through its rear end! These plump nymphs are voracious feeders and have a special way of catching their prey — their lower lip covers their entire face like a mask and extends out like a scoop! Their food includes other aquatic insects, tadpoles and tiny fish.

As you crawl over the rocks, some of the small green, worm-like Caddisfly larvae may attach to you. (It feels like a little pin prick.) They live in tiny nets like bits of nylon stocking attached to rocks (sometimes by the millions) and also live under rocks in tube-like cases of sand or twigs. See if you can find a surface without Caddisfly "nets" ... they are everywhere ... except in deep or still water.

Carefully lift the plate-size rocks in shallow, fast-moving water to find the slow-moving predatory Hellgrammites. With your face under water, watch them walk through very fast current holding on with their many sharp legs. (They may crawl on your hand if you stay still, but can pinch you if you pick them up!) Hellgrammites eat other nymphs and are in turn a favorite food of bass.

Crayfish — Crayfish look like little lobsters and in Louisiana big ones are eaten. The two claws hold and tear dead creatures which are their food. While they normally walk forward, they will scoot away backwards when alarmed. The female carries her eggs and young under her tail. In the river they are small: a half inch in the first year and one inch or so in the second ... and then they get eaten. Place a crayfish in a face mask full of water to watch it move. Look for eggs. If left a few minutes with a worm, it will usually catch and eat it.

Young Smallmouth Bass — Look in pools and behind rocks. It has red eyes and a yellow dot on the tail.

Darter — Look under rocks. It walks on its fins.

Satinfin Shiner — Look in potholes. It resembles a guppy.

Bull Chub — Look for fish forming schools. Underwater it has a dark line with a gold line along the side. This is the most common kind of fish in the river — and one of two that eat clams!

Sunfishes — Many kinds. Look for a dark dot on the gill cover.

Channel Catfish — Look for smooth skin, forked tail and "whiskers" on face (barbels) used to taste the river mud; can be large.

Smallmouth Bass — The most popular game fish. It has red eyes and dark stripes on the sides; can be large. Babies have a yellow tail.

Vintage Morrie and Susannah Piersol

American Eel — Snake-like fish seems to "bite" water to breathe and may be found in rocky cracks and "caves."

Carp — Silver or slightly yellow and heavy bodied with big scales and tiny whiskers on the mouth.

Longnose Gar — Look for black dots on the sides of this long and slender fish. It usually stays still and then moves away very fast near the surface.

Stand on your head under water and pull your face close up to rocky overhangs. (It's spooky, but you'll often come face to face with a large fish.) Swim up into a stand of water willows in one foot of water and wait quietly with half of your mask above water and half below. (Breathe with a snorkel.) Lie in a shallow rapid (six inches deep) with your arms out to either side and small fish will often use you as their new territory! ≈

Victor Sorrell, former Principal of Hermitage Technical High School, with an April-caught shad from the rapids beneath the 14th Street Bridge. Jo Murphy, Communications and Program Coordinator of VCU's Department of Forensic Science, and JJ, English Setter, don't fish, but do enjoy walking and accompanying Victor.

Travis Hall, Product Manager for the Portland, Oregon-headquartered Stages Cycling, moved to RVA from Portland and continues to work remotely. He is a huge fan of the cycling trails along the James River. When asked his opinion of the Skills Area on Belle Isle he smiled and replied, "It's GREAT!" He is pictured here with his son, Julian, and you can see more of them by Googling Travis Hall Stages Cycling.

Night of the Living
February, 1995

It's the dark of night in late February and I'm a midnight hunter. I walk alone on the skinny Riverside Drive. Rain clouds part and reveal a patch of stars. I hear the roar of the Pony Pasture rapids a hundred yards downstream.

I've never seen a Spotted Salamander, but Ralph White told me they're here. He saw them two midnights ago in icy ditch water. Canada Geese honk out in the river. I point my spotlight but don't find them. They're big, salamanders are small.

I come to a roadside ditch on my left — shallow water in it, a fallen oak trunk across it. I balance on the trunk and shine my light into the water. It's a foot deep and clear — soupy with leaves and twigs and slimy-looking stuff. And it's not writhing with Spotted Salamanders.

Throughout my life I've been a sucker for wild goose chases if they have anything to do with water or fish. During our New York years I dragged JC to the December Hudson River sewer outlet on the midtown edge of Manhattan to cast lures for rumored stripers that supposedly wintered there. Nothing. I once poled the Alabama coast's midnight shallows with a beacon looking for theoretical flounder. Nothing. Growing up in Nashville I bicycled all the way to Richland Creek to catch the huge carp that supposedly swarmed beneath the railroad bridge. All I encountered was a hobo with a can of Vienna Sausages and a smoky fire. And during a business trip to California I took a 20-mile detour to wet a line in the legendary Lake Castaic where the next world-record bass was thought to live. Nada.

Nobody cared to accompany me tonight. JC is home in bed reading, Thomas is on the couch watching late-night television, and Kelly had better be off the phone by now. "I'm going out to look for Spotted Salamanders," was my goodbye. They didn't flinch.

I see one! There it is! Just like Ralph said. It's down there on the leaves in about eight inches of water. Just sitting there. But I don't see spots. It just looks pink, maybe five or six inches long.

There's another! I steady my light's beam. Three of them now, each about six inches, half body, half tail. They sort of writhe together — the mating dance. The male will deposit his sperm on the bottom of the pool and the female will pick it up in her cloaca. A salamander swims to the surface towards my light, sticks his nose out of the water, and then swims back down with a side to side undulation.

Now I see minnows — ones and twos and threes, greenish-gray, a half-inch to an inch and a half. My light doesn't bother them; they just slowly swim along. The cold air turns my breath into thick smoke through the flashlight's beam; I'm in a Twilight Zone.

This is a vernal pool: watered by early spring rains, but dry the rest of the year. Spotted Salamanders live in the woods in moist underground burrows and crawl hundreds of yards a night to get to vernal pools to breed. After a few days they crawl back.

I move to the other end of my oak trunk and find a bonanza: five Spotted Salamanders — big ones, maybe seven inches. And now I see the spots: two rows of pink spots on their brown skins. (Only later when I net one and remove it from the water do I find that the coloring is actually black with yellow spots. The stained midnight water distorts their apparent coloring.) Their heads are as large as the tip of my ring finger. And I can see their little black eyes on the sides of their heads. I clearly see all four legs — two just behind the head and two more a few inches back.

Now I see more minnows. Tadpoles too. Huge tadpoles. Bullfrog tadpoles, still in early stages, no legs sprouting yet. As big as my thumb. A dozen or more, some sitting motionless in the water, tilted with their heads upwards.

This ditch is filled with life, and its champions are the Spotted Salamanders. During their nighttime migration they have dodged and hid from all sorts of predators. Migration routes of Spotted Salamanders often include crossing roads, and their carnage feeds early morning birds. I look long at these creatures. I wonder if anyone else anywhere in this midnight world is also looking at salamanders. What other curiosities are happening?

I walk back to my car, turn on the headlights, pull out slowly from the parking spot and round the first curve. A giant owl startles me as he lifts from a low tree in the glare of the lights and banks his wings into the woods. ≈

The World of Algae

(Taken from a brochure written by Ralph White and published by the James River Park System)

Anyone can see birds, most people can spot fish and turtles, and a few can find aquatic insects. But can you find primitive life forms? The river offers a chance to examine very simple plantlife, prehistoric stuff, living threads that link us to the time before the dinosaurs!

Individual algae plants range in size from single cells to large mats of dense growth. You won't need a microscope to locate the following treasures, but a mask and snorkel are recommended. Good places to start include the shallows at Pony Pasture and 42nd Street.

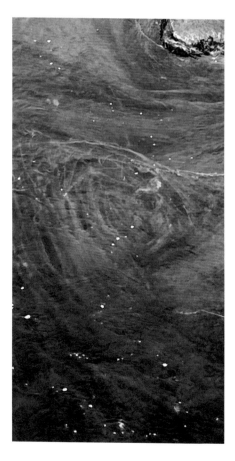

Wire Algae (Chara Zeylancia or Nitella Flexilis — very common) — Looks like a layer of frayed, plastic potscrubber. Forms mats an inch or two thick of short, tough, tangled stems. They feel like wiry roots. Find it attached to big rocks in fast, shallow water. Close-up inspection will reveal the larvae of insects, especially a kind of caddis fly. If you drag yourself over the tough algae mats, some of these larvae will attach to you, sometimes under your swimsuit. Tan or greenish in color, a quarter-inch long, and no thicker than a pencil lead, they hang on with tiny claspers at head and tail, but don't hurt.

Filamentous Green Algae or "Mermaid's Hair" (Spyrogyra) — Looks like hair in your hands. Underwater it appears to be a green cloud. Find it in shallow water — six inches down to a foot. A good place to find this algae is in the watery potholes in the Dry Rocks area. Reach your hand gently under a cloud of spirogyra and you'll often hit a thermocline — the boundary with a much cooler layer of water.

Jelly Algae (Tetraspora) — Looks like globules of mint jelly — clear, bright green spheres between the size of a dime and a quarter. Sometimes free-floating, other times in groups attached to cobbles one to two feet underwater. Prefers cool, slow-moving water with a sandy or gravely bottom. This algae is an indicator species of non-polluted water. It is highly susceptible to damage from fast water, but grows back quickly.

Felt Algae (Fagus longicauda) — Looks like a soft, furry layer a half-inch thick or less; usually brown on top and black underneath. A sample can be carefully lifted up to reveal a crumbly texture like rotted leather. Sometimes there is a thin skin of dark green on top which is another kind of algae. It sometimes smells like wet bread. Other times it has a "sewage" smell which comes from the anaerobic decomposition of the algae cells on the bottom of the felt mat. This algae can be an indicator of polluted water. Find it coating big rocks, up to five feet down, at the mouth of Reedy Creek by the James River Park System headquarters. If you have any open cuts or sores, wash them off after handling this yucky algae. ≈

Brandi Walker (right), who moved to RVA from NC, and Britt (declined to give last name), who moved here from Northern VA, enjoy all of James River Park and the festivals along the river, including the VA PrideFest.

Annual Events

~~~~~~~~~~

Although there are daily activities and events along the urban James River, listed here is a sampling of the events that happen annually. (The author of this book welcomes suggestions for additional annual events to be included in a future edition of this book: jbryanfish@aol.com.)

Jim Bland, owner and co-founder of RVA's beloved Plan 9 Music, at the annual riverside Richmond Folk Festival where Plan 9 offers recordings of many of the Festival's performers.

Crabs & Beer by the James

(crabsandbeerbythejames.com)

This noon-until-nine event is an all-you-can-eat crabs and beer festival on Brown's Island. It features live music, craft beers, and specialty food vendors. Lawn chairs and blankets are welcome. ≈

Vintage Thomas Bryan with fresh catch of crabs below the 14th Street Bridge.

Dominion Energy RiverRock

(riverrockrva.com)

Located on Brown's Island and surroundings, this is "the nation's premiere outdoor sports and music festival." Events for both local and national competitors include bouldering, trail running, mountain biking, air dogs (leaping into a pool), kayaking, stand-up paddleboarding, photography, video, fishing, and more. Co-presented by Venture Richmond and Sports Backers, the three-day event showcases "Richmond's unique riverfront, downtown trails, and whitewater rapids to residents of the region and visitors from around the country." Riverrock includes lots of pop-up events as well as free opportunities to try kayaking, standup paddleboarding, bouldering, slacklining and more. Plus, there is an abundance of family-friendly exhibitors and food/drink opportunities. ≈

▶ PICTURED RIGHT (TOP): Every year amateur photographer Sue Berinato participates in the Dominion Energy Riverrock photo competition along the river in downtown Richmond.

Friday Cheers

Presented by Venture Richmond, this is a summer music series that "brings some of the biggest up-and-coming artists to Brown's island at the best price for a family-friendly night of live music and fun for all ages." The event's every-slice-of-life crowd can enjoy food and beverage vendors, a sprinkling of exhibitors (including some with activities for children), very loud music up close OR carry-on-a-pleasant-conversation music at the other end of the island. Picnic blankets and lawn chairs are standard equipment. ≈

◂ PICTURED LEFT: Richmonders LaTonya Whitaker (UVA health worker originally from San Diego and Virginia Beach), Capital One employee Rick Plautz (originally from Utah) and children Olivia Hager and George Plautz, enjoy the family-friendly Friday Cheers on Brown's Island.

Tricia Pearsall's Suggestions for Newcomers

Tricia Pearsall has given longtime volunteer energies working and advocating for the welfare of the river and James River Park. Although paddling and fishing top her personal enjoyment list, she welcomes opportunities to snow-shoe in the Park. Her top suggestions for newcomers to the urban river? Walk on the Pipeline and the T-Pott Bridge, explore the Wetlands, and visit Pump House Park.

106

James River Regional Cleanup

This annual event, coordinated by JRAC (James River Advisory Council — info on Facebook), takes place on a Saturday in September during James River Week and includes several cleanup sites in the Richmond area. ≋

James River Week

This week-long September celebration throughout the James River's watershed features a variety of different events each year in Richmond such as sturgeon-watching on a pontoon boat out of Rocketts Landing, volunteer clean-up opportunities, family field day on Belle Isle, etc. "Whether volunteering, experiencing your first batteau trip, participating in a paddle adventure, or devouring delicious oysters, we encourage you to spend some time this week connecting with the James and your fellow river-lovers." Details: thejamesriver.org ≋

Jampacked Craft Beer & Music Festival

(jampackedfestival.com)

This music event on Brown's Island showcases the products of craft breweries and cideries. ≋

King of the James

Want an ultimate test of your multi-faceted skills and stamina? Every fall the James River Outdoor Coalition (JROC) presents a formidable opportunity: the "King of the James" event. The event is composed of challenging routes that require biking, running and paddling — all along Richmond's James River. Anyone can enter; details at jroc.com. The following excerpts from JROC's website will give you glimpses of what's in store for competitors.

"A Le Mans-style start will kick off the event. When the flag drops, riders will run across the parking lot to their bikes, jump on ..."

"Continue running in the creek and under the railroad tracks using a second set of culverts. Hop out of the creek before you run into the James. Make your way to the boats staged at Reedy Creek Meadow."

"At this point, you have made it through the mountain bike and trail run portion of the 'King of the James.' You're tired. You're exhausted. Now you will have to descend the James River and its many difficult rapids ... 1st Break, Approach, Corner, Hollywood, Hollywood Shoals, X's, 2nd Break (ferry towards Pipeline), Pipeline."

"Relax and sit back. Take a breather. You just finished the 'King of the James.'" ≈

LGBTQ+

Heralded in an article by Stuart Elliott in *The New York Times*, OutRVA is Richmond Region Tourism's award-winning campaign to highlight the area, including the James River Park System, as a welcoming destination for LGBTQ+ visitors. The "Family Fun" section of the website, www.outrva.com, includes river-related locations such as Belle Isle. And the annual VA Pridefest celebration often takes place on Brown's Island in downtown Richmond.

◄ PICTURED LEFT: Joseph Curtis (left, Department of Defense) and Darrin McCloskey (restaurant mgr.) live in Norfolk but come to RVA often to enjoy the river and the festivals — such as the VA Pridefest.

James River Parade of Lights, Holiday Boat Parade

Coordinated by the James River Advisory Council (JRAC), this December event features a variety of boats decorated with holiday lights — "parading" on the James River including in the Rocketts Landing area. ≈

Que Pasa Festival
(quepasafestival.com)

This family-friendly annual riverfront event showcases the diversity and beauty of Hispanic and Latin American cultures through music, food, visual and performing arts, and a variety of activities. ≈

▲ PICTURED ABOVE: Left to right at RVA's Que Pasa Festival: Meta professional R.J. Simmons and small business owner Desiree Ramos live in Prince George. Homemaker and RVA native Marshall Jewett and his fiancée Lee Maforah, a nurse who moved to RVA 4 years ago from Alabama, live in Beaverdam. They all enjoy the entire James River Park System.

Richmond Folk Festival
(richmondfolkfestival.org)

As per the website: "The Richmond Folk Festival is one of Virginia's largest events, drawing visitors from all over the country to downtown Richmond's historic riverfront. The Festival is a FREE three-day event ... features performing groups representing a diverse array of cultural traditions on seven stages." At the annual Festival expect to find hundreds of thousands of persons representing every slice of life — all happily tapping their toes to music. ≈

Richmond International Dragon Boat Festival

This annual event presented by Sports Backers welcomes corporate and community teams. "Richmond's biggest spectacle on water! Led by the rhythmic beat of a

drum, teams of 20 synchronized paddlers, one drummer and one steersperson, race 500 meters up the river in 40-foot canoes rigged with decorative Chinese dragon heads and tails. From vets to newbies, anyone can have a good time — plenty of time to kick back (or throw down!) between races." ≈

Run Richmond 16.19

(runrichmond1619.org)

Run Richmond 16.19 is part of the annual **AFRICA RECONNECT Event Series** that the Djimon Hounsou Foundation initiated in 2022. "The events aim to symbolically reverse the direction of the slave trade, showcase how the past is connected to the present and future, and celebrate Unity in Diversity." Much of the Richmond route takes place along the river and includes places where enslaved Africans arrived in Richmond, were jailed and sold, and from which they were shipped "down south." The route also includes monumental artworks such as the Emancipation and Freedom monument on Brown's Island. ≈

RVA Duck Race and Festival of Inclusion

Held on Brown's Island in 2022 (and hopefully to take place in future years) and hosted by the Autism Society of Central Virginia, this is a free, sensory-friendly festival designed to include

individuals with autism and other developmental disabilities. It includes music, family activities, and thousands of plastic ducks racing down the canal. ≈

▸ PICTURED RIGHT: Originally from Pennsylvania and then Illinois, Steve (former microbiology professional and now a stay-at-home dad), Megan (clinical psychologist at McGuire VA Medical Center), and four-year-old Milo Enders experience the T-Pott Bridge.

Enjoying the Festival of Inclusion on Brown's Island: John Nemetz (red shirt), Neville Morrison (black), Priscilla Nemetz (pink), Chrystal Hall (camo), Kaysen Nemitz (dino), Tonia Nemetz (white), Stella Payne (lavender), and Lincoln Payne (dino, blue glasses).

Inclusion

That word, "inclusion," has a special meaning to those of us who have involvements with the world of physical and intellectual disabilities such as Down Syndrome, cerebral palsy, autism spectrum disorder, and on and on and on. We've found that Richmond's James River, including its woods and waters and trails and activities, is not only welcoming, but is also nourishing and even therapeutic.

RVA Reggae Jerk Fest
(rvareggaejerkfest.org)

Held each summer on Brown's Island, this family-friendly event offers an afternoon and evening of live Reggae performances and Jamaican style jerk cuisine. "Reggae music is love that the world can enjoy. We celebrate the diverse community of Richmond. People from all races and cultures come to celebrate the oneness of humanity." ≈

RVA Street Art Festival

(rvastreetart.com)

This multi-day festival that celebrates the growth of street art in Richmond doesn't happen every year, but when it does it often focuses on the Haxall Canal area (the Canal Walk near 12th and Byrd Streets). The Festival's primary attraction is the painting of murals — happening on huge outdoor walls as the Festival takes place. There are also food and drink vendors, music, and other activities. ≈

VA Pridefest

(vapride.org)

This free and family-friendly event, located on Brown's Island in 2022, features entertainment, food, specialty vendors, and a variety of activities. Produced by VirginiaPride, this is the organization's annual celebration of LGBT communities. ≈

Wood River Run

(jamesriverpark.org)

This annual family-friendly 5K walk/run, organized by Friends of James River Park, is in honor and memory of Christian Wood, a young kayaker who lost his life paddling on the river in 2018. A portion of the proceeds from the run funds scholarships to Passages Adventure Camp. The run takes place each spring at Pony Pasture Rapids — one of the most beautiful sections of James River Park. ≈

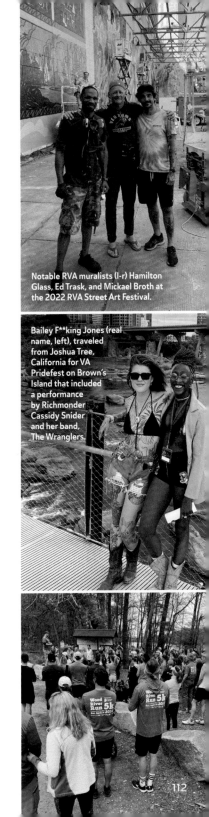

Notable RVA muralists (l-r) Hamilton Glass, Ed Trask, and Mickael Broth at the 2022 RVA Street Art Festival.

Bailey F**king Jones (real name, left), traveled from Joshua Tree, California for VA Pridefest on Brown's Island that included a performance by Richmonder Cassidy Snider and her band, The Wranglers.

VCU health sciences student Princess Otabil and VCU communications student Jasmine Wagner, enjoy other areas of the river including Texas Beach and Belle Isle.

Much More

The following section indeed provides "much more," and it's the section where, if there were room for a few hundred more pages, I would write about things such as crabbing in late summer beneath the 14th Street Bridge, gathering golf balls in the shoreline waters just downstream from the Wetlands, descriptions of the fascinating geology of the river, full lists of the urban river's wildflowers and birds, interviews with our Mayor and Governor, and so MUCH more. But hopefully the following entries in this guidebook will be satisfactory for now.

Poetry Along the River

One of Ralph White's many-years-ago publications, funded by Friends of James River Park, is entitled, "Poetry Guide to the James River Park System." The little booklet contains a variety of poetry by masters such as Emerson and MacLeish and by lesser-knowns and including Haiku and Cinquain. The booklet also has blank pages for one's own writings. The booklet's instructions are straightforward.

1. Select and go to a specific location (maps are included).
2. Observe for a few minutes.
3. Read a poem (from the booklet).
4. "Stay still and contemplate the meanings."
5. "Write a poem, reflections or musings." One of the poems in the booklet is by Edna St. Vincent Millay: "Earth does not understand her child, / Who from the loud gregarious town / Returns, depleted and defiled, / To the still woods, to fling him down." I vote for more of us to write our own poetry guides for our urban river. ≈

JC Gilmore-Bryan

The Secret Spot that Nobody Else Knows

There's a secret spot along the Richmond portion of the James River that I believe no-body else knows about yet. I discovered it when I moved to Richmond back in 1981 and it's as undiscovered today as it was back then.

It's a lot like that Beach Boys song written by Scott McKenzie and Mike Love: "Kokomo." ***"That's where you wanna go to get away from it all ..."*** When JC and I go there, ***"we'll perfect our chemistry, and by and by we'll defy a little bit of gravity ..."***

The James River Park System includes 600+ acres not including the river itself with its sandy shallows, sunbathing boulders, multi-size islands, and countless currents. In 2022 there were two million visits to this national BEST of urban waterways. But my and JC's secret spot, as far as I can tell, remains a secret. ***"That dreamy look in your eye gives me a tropical contact high."***

Bryce Wilk, former Park Superintendent for Richmond, gave me an unexpected suggestion for this guidebook. He said that I shouldn't reveal all of the river's secrets, that I shouldn't deprive the book's readers from discovering some of them for themselves. As you'll see, this book provides lots of information — much of it about little-known things. But it doesn't reveal all of the river's secrets. Possibly hundreds await your personal discovery. And you may decide, as JC and I have, to keep one secret spot just for yourself.

Thus, with my apologies, I'll keep my own little spot a secret just for JC and me: ***"We'll get there fast and then we'll take it slow. That's where we wanna go ..."***

The James River in Richmond beckons: ***"Come on pretty mama ..."*** ≈

Wheelchair and Stroller Accessibility

Many of the paths and trails and venues of the James River in Richmond are wheelchair friendly. And thanks to public and private funding as well as advocacy and volunteer energies, wheelchair accessibility continues to increase. Most notable is the Universal Access Ramp at the Huguenot Flatwater section of the river — an area of the river that is calm and rapids-free. The new ramp makes it easy for anyone to get on and off the river.

Throughout this guidebook you'll find information about accessibility. The section about the trails, for example, describes each trail's accessibility.

The largest section of James River Park, Belle Isle, is a wonderful example of accessibility. It can be reached from either shoreline by bridge, and the island's main loop is barrier free and includes three concrete ramps that go right down to the water.

Likewise, the Canal Walk is another accessible location and includes not only historical signage and artifacts, but also artworks and statues.

Brown's Island, accessible by three bridges, is an everyone's-welcome site for an abundance of festivals, performances, and events of all kinds. And the south side of the island provides access to perhaps the most engaging views of the river: the T. Tyler Potterfield Memorial Bridge which spans the entire river atop gorgeous rapids afloat with kayaks and tubes and standup paddleboards.

Explore, ask for assistance when needed, and let your voice be heard if you have suggestions: James River Park System headquarters: (804) 646-6443. ≈

Scott Dickens (Co-Founder of Rocket Pop Media) on Accessibility

1. Do research; there are great maps of the trails.

2. Let Friends of James River Park know if you want additional access.

3. Belle Isle is wonderful!

Sally Wetzler and the Access Ramps

Sally Wetzler uses the term "shepherded" when she talks about her role in establishing the accessible ramps at Reedy Creek and Huguenot Flatwater. But she is credited by others as THE person whose work and perseverance resulted in the ramps, and she's the star of Dominion Energy Charitable Foundation's video (featured on their website) about the Huguenot Flatwater Universal Access Ramp. Sally was introduced to kayaking in 1995, many years after her spinal cord injury, and she was immediately hooked. In spite of significant mobility issues, she is an avid kayaker, including whitewater. Her home water is Richmond's James River, but she kayaks on many other waters from Mexico to Canada to Utah, and on and on.

For the recently completed Huguenot Flatwater Universal Access Ramp project, initiated by JROC, Sally had lead roles in fundraising, advocacy and City relationships. "It's a great example of a public/private partnership," Sally confirms as she praises the City's involvement and its commitment of significant resources.

She is quick to point out that the river's access ramps aren't just to accommodate paddling, and aren't just for persons who use wheelchairs. The ramps are for access to the water (without having to climb down a steep bank, for example): for families with babies and toddlers, for persons who use canes or walkers, for anglers, etc. And she advises (from experience) that you shouldn't assume that a certain area can never be accessible; there may be a variety of ways to make it accessible. And finally, she deplores the term "wheelchair-bound;" her chair is her freedom. (To see a video of Sally, go to the Dominion Energy Charitable Foundation's website and search "Sally Wetzler.")

▲ PICTURED ABOVE: The Smiths: Jana, Jason and children Lola (7), Beau (3), and Wilder (1), enjoy a dirty activity at the Dominion Energy Riverrock display of the Virginia Composting Council — under the supervision of volunteer Bonnie Mahl. "We always come to Riverrock," smiled Jason — "and we love the trails," added Jana. "And the nearby breweries," continued Jason.

Children's Activities

There are hundreds of activities that children can enjoy along Richmond's James River. If you're interested in organized opportunities, take a look at the ANNUAL EVENTS and COMPANIES AND ORGANIZATIONS sections of this book. Most of the events are family-friendly and have plenty of opportunities for children to be engaged. And several of the companies and organizations offer classes, instruction and camps for children.

Next examine the PLACES section of this book and you'll no doubt see places that you know are just right for your children. One example is the T-Pott Bridge which is visually engaging for all categories of children — children in back- and front-packs and strollers as well as children on foot and wheel. The bridge offers an easy walk as well as an exhilarating run, and its railing system provides complete safety while not being visually obstructive.

An easy-access area for playing in the sand and shallow waters is Tredegar Beach. For a non-crowded, easy-parking walk along wooded trails, the Wetlands is a great place. For rock-hopping and nature-loving you can't beat the Dry Rocks. Easy-access fishing is available at Rocketts Landing Wharf. Biking children, from toddlers to experts, will greatly enjoy the Skills Area on Belle Isle. And for snorkel children, you can't go wrong with Pony Pasture. Older children who are interested in history will enjoy the historic signage all along the river. A good place to start is the group of 22 bronze medallions along the Canal Walk. And of course a walk on the Slave Trail reveals the city's greatest shame.

Following is a list of specific activities that children can enjoy the river.

Nature Bingo — Make a bingo grid that lists things that can be found along the river such as animal tracks, skeletons (snakes and turtles, mammals, etc.), acorns, feathers (sizes/colors), wildflowers (colors), berries (colors), hickory nuts, mushrooms, etc. Caution the children that they are not to collect them, but merely mark the bingo sheet when they find them. (Natural things along the river are to be left for everyone to enjoy.)

Litter Scavenger Hunt — (Sadly, some litter does exist along the river.) Give the child a garbage bag (and perhaps plastic gloves) along with a list of specific types of litter: can, broken glass, shoe, item of clothing, plastic bag, bottle top, piece of metal, broken toy, fishing line, etc.

Bottle Cap Collection — Occasionally you may encounter areas where people regularly litter with bottle caps. You may want to give a prize to the child who collects the greatest variety. (Plastic gloves are suggested for this activity.)

Nature Journal — Provide a small sketchpad and color pencils for the child and encourage drawings of things of interest: a pretty leaf, vines on a tree trunk, boulders in the river, etc.

Nature Identification — Get readily available apps for your mobile phone

MUCH MORE

so your child can identify flowers, plants, trees and animal tracks.

Shelling — There is a variety of mollusk shells (snails, mussels, etc.) along the river. Children can find them and take photos to identify later via the Internet or guidebook.

Collaborative Storytelling — You and your child tell a story together taking turns. In advance prepare several prompts with which you can begin the stories, such as, "A little boy was walking along a trail in the woods when he suddenly saw a _____."

Rock Art — In many places there are rocks of all sizes along the river's shorelines. Children can stack and pile and arrange the rocks into compelling artworks.

Leaf Mandala — In the fall when the leaves transform into beautiful colors, children can place them on the ground in colorful patterns: concentric circles, rainbows, etc.

Wooden Boats — Children can pick up sticks or pieces of bark and float them as boats. Where there is some current they can have races.

Vintage Kelly and Thomas Bryan

Bucket And Shovel — You can't go wrong by going to a watery area and handing a child a plastic beach bucket and shovel. Then just sit back and watch. ≈

Dogs

Dog owners will find that most of the public areas — unless otherwise designated by signage — along the urban James River are extremely welcoming to dogs. One dog-favorite spot is the Pony Pasture area. The immediate area can be crowded, but if you walk east along the river trail for a fourth of a mile you'll encounter Half Moon Beach which is popular for dogs. And further downstream is the Wetlands area that has much calmer water that is great for splashing. North Bank Park (aka Texas Beach) has a relatively long walk downhill to the river, but it is much less crowded than more accessible areas and there are plenty of riverside areas for dogs to enjoy. Belle Isle is extremely popular for dogs and is large enough that even on best weekend days you can still find secluded, uncrowded areas. Just be careful along the northern side of the island where there are rapids that are dangerous for dogs.

Be aware that a City of Richmond ordinance states that dogs must be leashed, tethered, or fenced. Dog owners should realize that dogs can create hazards for hikers and bikers on the trails and that for some persons, especially some children, dogs can be threatening. Plus, an unleashed dog in the James River Park may interact with potentially dangerous animals such as snakes, raccoons, and foxes. And finally, another Richmond City Ordinance requires that dog owners pick up excrement from their dogs. ≈

▲ PICTURED ABOVE: Richmonder Lindsey Faulkner works as a library assistant at Falling Creek Middle School and is also a library science student at Old Dominion University. She and four-year-old Chema, seen here on the Low Line, also enjoy Chapel Island.

▼ PICTURED BELOW: Creative director Jon Horn, seen here with his best friend Nico, moved to RVA from New York a few years ago to get away from New York's COVID immersion.

Isabel Levengood,

pictured here with her Boxer/Pitbull Nalu, finds the trails along the James River to be dog friendly. She says that Pony Pasture and Belle Isle are where you'll see the most dogs and are great places for them to socialize.

122

VCU art student Caroline Matranga and VCU marketing student Erika Waszak, pictured here at Tredegar Beach, also enjoy Belle Isle, Texas Beach, and other areas of the urban James.

Petersburg residents Lucifer Gray and Laura Johnson enjoy fishing in the lock at Great Shiplock Park. Lucifer is a writer of horror/suspense (Poe is his favorite), and Laura is a manager for Food Lion. I asked Lucifer if he has gotten any writing ideas while here: "Yes, [long pause] about what's on the end of her line." Laura raised her eyebrows and smiled.

Views of the River

The best overlooks of the river are from tall buildings, bridges, and the south shoreline Floodwall. But there are four other views that merit mention.

Riverview Cemetery — Enter the cemetery at the corner of Colorado and Randolph and drive to the south side of the cemetery to River Crescent Way. There are good winter views of the river, but an abundance of foliage obscures summer views.

Libbie Hill Park — This nicely manicured little park, at the corner of N. 29th and Libbie Hill Terrace, provides a very nice downstream view of the river — the view that is similar to the view of England's Richmond Upon Thames, and that was (anecdotally) the inspiration for naming our city Richmond.

Oregon Hill Overlook — At the corner of South Pine and Oregon Hill Parkway, there are great views of the river in winter, but summer views are not so good due to the foliage.

Hollywood Cemetery — Enter the cemetery at the corner of South Cherry and Albemarle Streets. The southeast border of the cemetery has nice views of the river, including one area with benches and another at a walk-around mausoleum. ≈

Jon Lugbill's Top Five Suggestions

1 At low water float from Pony Pasture to Reedy Creek.

2 At low water explore the rocks adjacent to the south side of Belle Isle.

3 Traverse the "Loop" (approx. 7 miles) — North Bank Trail on the north side of the river, then across to the Buttermilk Trail on the south side, then back to north.

4 Walk on the Pipeline — especially in April when there is an abundance of fish and Great Blue Herons and Eagles.

5 Enjoy sunrise on the T. Tyler Potterfield Memorial Bridge.

Atlantic Sturgeon

The Atlantic sturgeon has become the poster fish of the James River. Although mostly downstream, sturgeon are now occasionally seen in the city, with the most notable sightings beneath the 14th Street Bridge. There are stories about there once being so many sturgeon in what is now downtown Richmond that you could almost walk across the river on their backs. Other stories say that a rite of passage for young Indians was to ride on the backs of sturgeon. As large as 14 feet and 800 pounds, Atlantic sturgeon spend their lives in the ocean and return to the river to spawn in spring and fall. Commercial harvesting was the major cause of the depletion of sturgeon populations in the late 1800s, after which additional challenges such as sedimentation and pollution continued the negative impact. Since 2006 several organizations, including the Richmond-headquartered James River Association and VCU's Rice Rivers Center, have worked together to restore a population

of sturgeon in the James River. The success can be seen by looking at the river in September from the fishing dock at Osborne Landing and/or from a boat most anywhere along the tidal mileage downstream from Richmond. It is no longer unusual to see giant sturgeon leaping completely out of the water in early fall, and sturgeon-watching boat trips are common. ≈

126

The Football Game on Mayo's Island

From the *Richmond Times-Dispatch*: "Richmond football patrons will see just about their last gridiron duel of the season this afternoon at Tate Field where the Arrow A.C. will come to grips with the Southern Athletic Club, independent champions of Washington, D.C."

There were no Washington Redskins or Commanders back in the 1920s when the *Richmond Times-Dispatch* covered this highly anticipated contest on Mayo's Island. Washington's teams had names like Mohawk and Apache, and of course their invincible champions that year, the Southern Athletic Club.

Several years ago the late Carlisle Butler, a native Richmonder, told me about that game. He was a tall man, but claimed he was one of the smallest players that year for Richmond's Arrow Athletic Club. He told me about the physical beating he took that day on that James River island.

The RTD: "Arrow, whether it wins or loses today, will wind up its greatest gridiron campaign in years. Arrow hasn't tasted defeat this season. It is a well-coached, smooth-working and swift-moving machine which has made life miserable for every opponent it has faced this year."

Butler's youthful James River experiences ranged well beyond football on Mayo's Island. He would trek through the woods and camp near Bosher's Dam. But mostly he liked observing things, and when he had the chance, drawing and painting them. His estate included one painting he completed when he was 12 — an uphill view from the banks of the James.

Today Mayo's Island is privately-owned and mostly unused. But 100 years ago the Island was the site of Tate Field where 5,000+ spectators

Riverside Meadow Greenspace

This 2-acre slice of land with 1,500 feet of frontage on the river, was donated to the city by John Pearsall. Located on Riverside Drive a half-mile upstream (northwest) from Pony Pasture, Riverside Meadow Greenspace provides no parking and can be reached only by walking/biking along Riverside Drive. Here's what visitrichmond.com says about it: "The area is well-attended by walkers, joggers, bikers, bird-watchers, fishermen and especially paddlers. Since the Z-Dam is connected to Riverside Meadow and Williams Island across the river, one can often find kayakers surfing in the powerful notch in the dam. The view of the James and Pony Pasture Rapids from the meadow is beautiful and a big draw for the little park. The patient wildlife watcher will find bald eagles, otters, osprey and great blue herons in this area. The mix of calm water to the left, rapids to the right and tall trees along both shorelines creates a rich mix of habitats."

gathered to watch Carlisle Butler and Richmond's Arrow Athletic Club take on the bigger, stronger "stalwart pigskin chasers from the National Capital."

That game was rough. It confirmed Butler's decision to switch from player to assistant manager the following year. And the beauty of nature that he saw and drew as a youngster along the James River confirmed his resolve to find his livelihood as an artist rather than athlete.

The Richmond Arrow, although outclassed and out-muscled, won that day on Mayo's Island: 8-0. Their highly-touted "Pony Express" backfield was stopped time after time — except for a 40-yard breakaway sprint for a touchdown by Alan Plunkett, "Arrow's rangy and crafty halfback ... the galloping back of the Pony Express." They missed the extra point. Later the Washington team mishandled a snap from center behind its goal line and yielded a two-point safety.

(Carlisle Butler discontinued football and went on to become a nationally recognized landscape architect and THE national authority on memorial park cemeteries — designing public and private thoroughfares, residences, gardens, office parks, and more than 400 cemeteries.) ≈

Richmond Riverfront Plan
(Can be found at rva.gov)

"The Richmond Riverfront Plan, adopted by Richmond City Council in November 2012 as a part of the City's Master Plan and Downtown Plan, is the City's vision document for the Riverfront. The plan covers both sides of the James River from Belle Isle to Rockett's (sic) Landing and outlines steps for the improvement of our Riverfront as a single unified, cohesive space. It discusses the Richmond Riverfront's unique history and makes recommendations for each section of the Riverfront. Finally, the plan establishes priorities for the Riverfront and outlines potential mechanisms for management of this unique place in our city." Author's note: If you read the Plan, you'll see that much is yet to be accomplished. Of course as soon as any strategic or master plan is adopted for anything, the landscape continues to change and thus the plan is continually subject to modification, reconsideration, and even drastic change and reversal. Nevertheless, the Richmond Riverfront Plan is evidence of the City's understanding and careful consideration of the river's unique importance for the vitality of the region. ≈

▼ PICTURED BELOW: Chris Frelke, Director of Richmond's Department of Parks, Recreation and Community Facilities and Richmond Mayor Levar Stoney.

James River Park System Master Plan

(Available for download at jamesriverpark.org)

The James River Park System's 87-page Master Plan, filled with charts and maps and photographs, was adopted by Richmond City Council in 2020 as a flagship project of Friends of the James River Park, and "to establish a single reference point for capital planning and future implementation, sustaining natural counterpoint to urban life, balancing both active recreation and passive enjoyment of the Park while preserving and protecting the natural environment." "The James River corridor has been repeatedly distorted by transport, industry, war, and severe pollution, each with a staggering scale and impact. Richmond residents have mobilized to swing the pendulum in the opposite direction, favoring conservation and recreation, acknowledging the intangible qualities of exploring the natural world have a restorative and transformational impact on one's health." Author's note: If you read the Plan, you'll see that much is yet to be accomplished. Of course as soon as any strategic or master plan is adopted for anything, the landscape continues to change and thus the plan is continually subject to modification, reconsideration, and even drastic change and reversal. Nevertheless, the James River Park System Master Plan is evidence of a broad swath of both public and private understanding and careful consideration of the James River Park's unique importance for the vitality of the region. ≈

▶ PICTURED RIGHT: James Harlow worked for Virginia State Parks for 7 years, and now works for the James River Park System for 3 years. He likes the varied tasks in the out of doors.

Rings

These are 2 of 8 17-foot, 2-ton rings that populate the paths leading to/from the southern entrance to the T. Tyler Potterfield Memorial Bridge. Created by artist Joshua Wiener, they are not only artworks to be individually interpreted by those who encounter them, but also a nod to the biking community and the wheelchair community which includes his father. The rings are along an extensive bike/hike/roll trail that, even with sharp turns and a steep hill, is completely barrier-free.

And, as stated in a *Richmond Magazine* article by Jackie Kruszewski, "They're meant to interact with the landscape over their 1,100-foot trek — the paths, climbing walls, historic artifacts and bridges that make up the James River Park System — but also with the people who use those amenities. The sculpture's patina will darken over time, as nature and humanity exert their influence. Go ahead: Stand inside, recreate da Vinci's Vitruvian Man drawing, take your selfies."

Greg Velzy's Five Suggestions

1. Get some basic instruction regarding swift water: maybe a two- or three-hour session or a little research on the web.

2. Get a map. Possible sources: the James River Park System, rvaMORE, and James River Outdoor Coalition (which has a bilingual map).

3. Leave no trace! This should be your prime consideration.

4. Enjoy the exploration/adventure aspect of the James River Park; you can find places and things that nobody else knows about.

5. Explore the history; there is an abundance of compelling signage.

99 Most Asked Questions About the Urban James

1. **What about snakes?** There are no poisonous water moccasins along the Richmond portion of the James River. Nobody has ever been harmed by any snake along the urban James.

2. **Are there really bald eagles in Richmond?** Sure, lots. You'll see them if you frequent the river.

3. **Is it okay to take home a pretty rock or nice piece of driftwood?** No. Every piece of nature along the river is protected: animals, flowers, driftwood, mushrooms, even the rocks. Leave all of it for everyone to enjoy.

4. **Can I safely go to the river alone?** This is an urban river and you should use the same precautions you might use anywhere else in the city. Although "muggings" are rare along the river, it's a good idea (and common sense) for women not to venture into isolated areas alone.

5. **Will my car be safe?** Use the same caution you would use anywhere else: leave something of value in a visible position and there's a slight chance of a broken window.

Joe Tierney (Columbia Gas), Kristen Erickson (graphic designer), Nolan (stroller) and Violette are originally from Yorktown, but moved to RVA from San Francisco. They are seen here enjoying the RVA Street Art Festival on Haxall Canal.

6. **Is it safe to swim?** Yes, with a few guidelines. Always wear shoes; the river is sprinkled with rebar and other manmade materials that can damage feet. Watch your children; there are no lifeguards. Don't wade or swim near swift water; it's more powerful than it looks and it can sweep you into a position of foot entrapment or body entrapment beneath undercut rocks and boulders.

7. **Is it safe to eat the fish?** Yes. There were serious problems many years ago, but all of the fish are now safe to eat.

8. **Do I need a fishing license?** Yes. A license can be purchased online from the Virginia Department of Wildlife Resources: dwr.virginia.gov

9. **Is it okay to camp along the river?** No.

10. **Is it okay to make a fire along the river?** No.

11. **Is it safe to go to the river at night?** James River Park is open only during daylight hours. But folks do enjoy other parts of the river at night — and during approved nighttime events in James River Park.

12. **Is there really a herd of albino deer?** No. There were reported sightings up until 1994.

13. **Is it okay to picnic along the river?** Of course. But glass containers are not allowed.

14. **Was there really a Civil War prison on Belle Isle?** Yes. It held up to 5,000 prisoners at a time.

15. **Can I take my dog?** Yes! Leashes and clean-up are required.

16. **Are there really Class V rapids in the city?** No. They are Class IV and lower. BUT, at certain high water levels, some are considered Class V.

17. **Have people really drowned in Hollywood Rapids?** Yes. Those rapids are safe only for experienced rafters and paddlers.

The Garber family (front to back): father Jon who is an engineer, daughter Isabelle who is celebrating her 19th birthday, her boyfriend Will Marden, mother Pennie who is an architect, Sadie who is a software developer, and Ben who is an economist, all live in Staunton, but came to Richmond to celebrate Isabelle's birthday, including painting with watercolors along the river.

18. **Can I keep the fish that I catch?** Yes, but there are size and number restrictions. Info can be found at dwr.virginia.gov

19. **Who maintains James River Park?** The James River Park System's staff is charged with maintaining the Park. But hundreds of volunteers under the auspices of a variety of organizations provide ongoing assistance.

20. **Were there Indians here?** Yes. When the first Europeans arrived in 1607 this was an important site for the Algonquians.

21. **Where is the best view of the river?** Hmmm, depends what you want. The T. Tyler Potterfield Memorial Bridge provides a wonderful water-level panorama. The south shore Floodwall provides a spectacular higher-up panorama. There are lots of "best" views; it's hard to find a bad view.

22. **Is this really the best smallmouth bass fishing in the nation?** No. If you mean numbers and sizes, it's not even close. But if you mean the ambience, it's hard to beat.

23. **Can you really catch herring on plain, unbaited, gold hooks?**
Yes. Drop a line below the 14th Street Bridge in April and you'll likely find out.

24. **Are there mammals on Belle Isle?** Yes. There are no deer, but muskrats, river otters, and red foxes have been sighted.

25. **Can I just inflate a tube and float on the river through the city?** Don't do it unless you are with someone who knows the routes. There are rapids that have taken lives.

26. **When were the canals built?** They were continually being built and maintained from the 1770s until the 1870s when the railroads took over.

Ryan Duckett, President of the Virginia Composting Council, met his wife at a meetup social at the Reedy Creek area of James River Park, just two weeks after he moved to Richmond. He enjoys paddling (Class II and below) and running the trails.

27. **What should I do if I see a problem in James River Park such as an obstructed trail, a pile of litter, or a dangerous fallen tree?** Contact the Park's office: (804) 646-6443.

28. **Are there any projects for volunteers in James River Park?** Yes, lots of organizations enlist volunteers to help in the Park. Start by calling the Park's office: (804) 646-6443.

29. **How can I get a detailed map of the urban James?** There are so many details that it's impossible for one map to contain

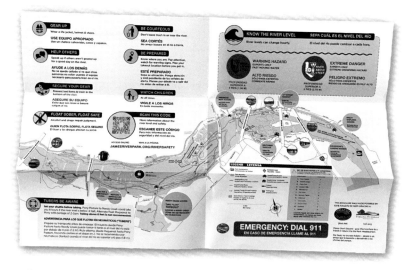

everything. James River Outdoor Coalition (jroc.net) produces a great map. But it's best to Google what you're looking for, such as a map for trails or a map for streets or a map for water routes, etc.

30. **Is it okay to drink the water?** Although the river is extremely clean, it's not a good idea to drink unprocessed water from any river or stream.

31. **Is it okay to take home a beautiful rock?** No. Leave every natural thing (flowers, leaves, sticks, etc.) for everyone to enjoy.

32. **How deep is the river?** At normal flow, upstream from the 14th Street Bridge it rarely gets over 5 feet deep, but downstream it reaches depths of 20 feet and more.

33. **Do high waters and floods wash away the fish?** No. They merely seek calm waters behind boulders and among inundated shorelines.

34. **When did settlers first arrive here?** The first Europeans arrived on May 24, 1607.

35. **What kinds of fish can you catch in the urban James?** Smallmouth bass, largemouth bass, crappie, blue catfish, channel catfish, flathead catfish, various sunfishes, herring, American shad, hickory shad, white perch, longnose gar, and a few others.

36. **How big is James River Park?** Approaching 600 acres at this writing.

37. **Is there much poison ivy along the urban James?** Yes! It has three leaves and its vines have little hairs that can hold onto tree bark.

38. **Can you eat the clams in the river?** It's not wise. The clams' filtering systems allow impurities to accumulate.

39. **What are those finger-size holes in some of the bigger rocks in the river?** They held fish traps and quarry equipment.

40. **How many prisoners were on Belle Isle?** 30,000 total, but no more than 5,000 at a time.

41. **Are there beaver dams along the urban James?** No. They make their dens under the banks of the river.

42. **What type of rock came from the Quarry Pond on Belle Isle?** Granite.

43. **Are there hummingbirds along the river?** Of course. They arrive in the Spring.

44. **Does the river ever get too crowded to float or paddle?** No. It's wide and is never too crowded.

45. **How high have floods gotten?** In 1972 Hurricane Agnes raised the river to 36.5 feet. Normal flow is less than 5 feet.

46. **Are there U.S. presidents buried in Hollywood Cemetery?** Two: James Monroe and John Tyler.

47. **Is the water deep enough to paddle during the lowest water in the summer?** Yes — even during the worst droughts.

48. **Why do they call it Hollywood Rapids?** From Hollywood Cemetery, which was named for the holly trees, that overlooks the river from the north.

49. **How deep is Belle Isle's Quarry Pond?** 19 feet.

50. **Do fish bite during the winter?** Downstream from the 14th Street Bridge, yes. Upstream, bites are few.

51. **How big do the fish get in the urban James?** Blue catfish occasionally reach 100+ pounds; stripers of 50+ pounds and largemouth weighing 10 pounds have been caught.

52. **Will gars bite you?** They won't bite you, although their toothy mouths look vicious.

53. **Can you fly-fish in the river?** Of course; it's perfect for fly-fishing.

54. **Is it okay to dive into the river in deep pools?** Bad idea. There are plenty of submerged rocks and manmade structures.

55. **Can I fish everywhere along the urban James at any time of the year?** Yes. Of course you need to avoid private property.

56. **Where can I rent a raft?** Hmmm. In the COMPANIES AND ORGANIZATIONS section of this book you can find places to rent kayaks and paddleboards and to book a ride on a raft. But the big rafts are not available to rent without a guide.

57. **What's the status of sturgeon?** They're back! They're readily seen leaping in the early fall a few miles downstream from Richmond, and are occasionally seen swimming in the tidal river between the 14th Street Bridge and the I-95 Bridge.

58. **What can you catch from the 14th Street Bridge?** In April you'll catch shad, stripers, and white perch. The rest of the year you'll catch mostly catfish.

59. **Is it good to fish near Great Blue Herons?** Yes. They stay where the fish are.

60. **Were there ever baseball games on Mayo's Island?** Yes, even Babe Ruth played exhibition games in the island's 7,000-seat stadium.

61. **Can fish go upstream past the rapids and the dams?** Yes. The final hurdle was Bosher's Dam, but its fish ladder now enables passage.

62. **How many species of birds can you commonly see along the river?** Well over 100.

63. **How many kinds of wildflowers grow along the urban James?** Newton Ancarrow listed 471 species.

64. **Does the river ever freeze?** It gets ice on it but almost never freezes all the way across.

65. **Can I take a beer to the river?** Alcohol is prohibited in James River Park.

66. **Does anyone live on Belle Isle?** No.

67. **Can I jet ski on the urban James?** Yes, downstream from the 14th Street Bridge, but there is a no-wake zone from the Bridge until well past Rocketts Landing. And yes upstream from Bosher's Dam.

68. **Where can I get a good guidebook on the urban James?** This is the only one (other than its predecessor that was published in 1997).

69. **Is there an organization I can join to help the welfare of the river?** Several, but start with these three: Friends of James River Park, JROC (James River Outdoor Coalition), and the James River Association.

70. **Are there fishing tournaments on the urban James?** No. But there are some upstream and downstream from Richmond.

71. **Are there concession stands or drink machines in James River Park?** No.

72. **Are there places to buy bait along the river?** No.

73. **Should I wear a pfd (personal flotation device) if I'm just wading?** Pfds are encouraged when the river level reaches 5 feet and higher. Below that, it's not necessary as long as you can swim and know to stay away from rapids.

Vintage
Thomas Bryan

74. What should I do if I see a snake? Leave it alone. There are no poisonous snakes along the urban James, and the snakes that do exist never harm anyone and are quite beneficial.

75. Can I wade barefoot? Not a good idea. There is broken glass, rebar, and other manmade debris.

76. Are there nude beaches? Not officially, but ask around.

77. Can you fish from any of the bridges? Yes, the 14th Street Bridge; it produces lots of fish during the month of April.

78. Is it okay to pick flowers? No. All natural things are protected and are to be left for everyone to enjoy.

79. What is the "Fall Line" and is it dangerous that Richmond is on it? The Fall Line is where the river's downhill path reaches tidal water

Physical therapist Janell Edwards enjoys sunbathing at her favorite spot along the urban James.

— beneath Richmond's 14th Street Bridge. There is nothing dangerous about Richmond being on the Fall Line.

80. Are there any trout in the river? Very rarely (one every several years) in Richmond.

81. Isn't the river poisoned by chemicals? Agricultural and industrial runoff affect many river systems, including the James, but the Richmond James is relatively "clean," and isn't "poisoned" enough to be harmful to recreational users or to the edibility of fish.

82. Is there a place where I can launch my motorboat? One place: Ancarrow's Landing.

83. Do they enforce the various No Parking signs along the river — such as those on Riverside Drive? YES!

84. Where are the best sunbathing spots? Pony Pasture and Belle Isle.

85. Is there any buried treasure along the urban James? None that we're aware of.

86. **Are there any good walking trails?** Yes, over 22 miles of them.

87. **Do I need hiking boots for the trails?** Wear whatever you're comfortable in. You'll see everything from high-top boots to sandals.

88. **Do they stock the river with fish?** In past years there have been initiatives with blue catfish and American shad, but nothing currently.

89. **How much is the entry fee to James River Park?** Zero.

90. **How many visits per year does James River Park get?** Over two million.

91. **How many attendees are counted at events each year on and around Brown's Island?** Over a million.

92. **What's the most popular annual event along the river?** The Richmond Folk Festival.

93. **I collect sea glass and river glass; is it okay to take home pieces of river glass that I find in the river?** Yes, please!

94. **How common is it to find arrowheads along the urban James?** Very rare.

95. **Where can I see river otters?** The better question is "When?" Although there are river otters, sightings are not common; best opportunities are at dawn.

96. **Does James River Park have anywhere that's wheelchair accessible?** Sure, lots of locations. Belle Isle is one of the great places.

97. **How does Richmond's James River rank nationally among river cities?** In 2012, after an extensive search and competition, *Outside Magazine* named Richmond the nation's best river city.

98. **Does the urban James have an official bird or fish?** Nothing official, but the Great Blue Heron and the Atlantic Sturgeon would get plenty of votes.

99. **Is it okay to ride my motorcycle in James River Park?** Sorry, but no. ≈

▸ PICTURED RIGHT, RIGHT IMAGE:
Jamal Boyd is able to access some areas of the urban James on his motorcycle.

Urban River Challenge

I'll put Richmond's James River up against any urban river in the nation based on its ability to deliver enjoyment, education, and inspiration — the EEI Quotient, EEIQ. To qualify as "urban" the river's city has to have its own airport as well as local television stations affiliated with NBC, ABC, and CBS. And you can consider only the area of the river that is within the city/metropolitan limits. Score the river by adding/subtracting points according to the following:

ALONG THE RIVER:

+ Add **5 points** if there is adequate (your judgment) public access.

+ Add **2 points** for each of the following that is adequately (your judgment) provided:

  + Picnic tables
  + Trash containers
  + Restrooms
  + Parking
  + Boat ramps and access
  + Signage (maps, rules, information)

+ Add **2 points** if technical rock climbing is common.

+ Add **2 points** if hiking and running are common.

+ Add **5 points** if there is adequate (your judgment) wheelchair access.

+ Add **2 points** if camping is allowed.

+ Add **2 points** if there are more than three miles of bike trails.

▼ PICTURED BELOW, LEFT IMAGE: Oil portrait painter Evelyn Horan, who recently moved to RVA from Maryland, and intaglio printmaker Ezra Heller, who is visiting from New York, examine interesting rocks in the urban river's currents. (Ezra shared that his grandfather is writer Peter Vassilopoulos who is an authority on islands and waterways on the Pacific coast.)

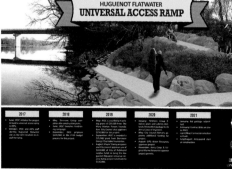

SWIMMING/BOATING:

+ Add **1 point** for each R month during which persons commonly swim.

+ Add **1 point** if scuba diving is common.

+ Add **1 point** if snorkeling is common.

+ Add **1 point** if there are paid lifeguards.

+ Add **1 point** for each R month during which persons commonly use watercraft.

+ Add **1 point** for each class of rapids (I through VI).

+ Add **1 point** if there are sailboats.

+ Add **1 point** if there are rowing crews.

FISHING:

+ Add **1 point** for each R month during which you can usually catch fish.

+ Add **1 point** for each species of fish that is abundantly caught.

+ Add **1 point** if fly-fishing commonly takes place.

− Subtract **3 points** if there are regulations prohibiting sale/consumption of any species of fish because of water quality.

NATURE

+ Add **2 points** if eagles are regularly seen.

+ Add **2 points** if antlered wildlife is regularly seen.

+ Add **2 points** if alligators are regularly seen.

+ Add **2 points** if the river is popular with birders.

+ Add **2 points** if there are designated nature trails.

+ Add **2 points** if there is descriptive signage regarding flora and fauna.

OTHER

+ Add **2 points** if there is descriptive signage regarding history.

+ Add **2 points** for each pedestrian bridge that crosses to the other side of the river or to a mid-river island.

− Subtract **3 points** if the river regularly (every 10 years or more often) floods into streets and/or buildings.

+ Add **3 points** if there is at least one nonprofit organization whose fundamental charge is the river's welfare.

− Subtract **2 points** if your river's level is dependent on the discharge of an upstream dam.

The EEIQ for Richmond's James River is 81. ≈

Eugene and Louise Hileman live in Portsmouth, but enjoy outings to Richmond simply to enjoy the river. Eugene is a physician's assistant and Louise is a retired nurse.

Parking

Although the river and its immediate surroundings, including the James River Park System, are the sites for wonderful activities, events, and opportunities, parking is limited. Following is a list of parking areas that are adjacent to river activities. But on weekends be prepared for these areas to be full and thereby having to search for parking elsewhere that sometimes requires a long walk.

South Side of the River
(listed from west to east):

Huguenot Flatwater — The entrance to this area is at the intersection of Riverside Drive and Southampton Street, and there is a large parking lot for 35+ cars. (See Huguenot Flatwater in the PLACES section of this book.)

Oxford — Just downstream from Huguenot Flatwater is a tiny parking area (9 cars) where Oxford meets Riverside. There is a path that leads into the woods and connects with the trails from Huguenot Flatwater.

Pony Pasture — Located at 7200 Riverside Drive is the 100-car parking lot for the Pony Pasture section of the James River Park System. The parking lot fills quickly on weekends, and additional nearby parking is scarce. (See Pony Pasture in the PLACES section of this book.)

Wetlands — Landria Drive deadends at the Wetlands section of the James River Park System, and there is a small "lot" that will hold 8 cars, and additional streetside parking for another 20 cars. Be careful with street parking; there is a deep ditch immediately adjacent to the pavement. (See Wetlands in the PLACES section of this book.)

Boulevard Bridge — Parking for southside access to Boulevard Bridge and the path that leads below the bridge is available on only a few streets near the top of the hill, thus requiring a long walk. The nearest parking street is Prince George (space for 30+ cars).

42nd Street — At the intersection of Riverside Drive and 42nd Street is a parking lot that holds 34 cars. This lot fills quickly on weekends. (See 42nd Street Entrance in the PLACES section of this book.)

Reedy Creek — At the intersection of Riverside and Hillcrest is the entrance to the parking area for the Reedy Creek section and headquarters of the James River Park System. The lot holds approximately 25 cars

▲ PICTURED ABOVE: Pictured here on the Footbridge to Belle Isle are Richmonder Jody Weaver (right), who works in business development, and new friend Savimiem Puaud, from France, who is doing an internship in Richmond.

and fills quickly on weekends. There is a bit of additional streetside parking in the general area. (See Reedy Creek Entrance in the PLACES section of this book.)

▲ PICTURED ABOVE: Jamal Boyd, a photographer and a chef at P.F. Chang, and Elijah Sanchez, who works at KFC, barefooting along the river. Jamal just moved back from Atlanta where he lived for six years, but he loves the nature of RVA: "I've been coming to the river forever!"

22nd Street — This entrance to James River Park is at the intersection of 22nd and Riverside and has room for 30+ cars. (See 22nd Street Entrance in the PLACES section of this book.)

21st Street (where it meets Riverside) — There is a kiosk, bridge, stairs, and path down to the Dry Rocks area that borders the south side of Belle Isle. There is street parking on 20th and 21st Streets for a dozen or more cars.

7th Street — At the intersection of 7th and Semmes is a 20-car parking lot that offers a path to the Floodwall Overlook and Floodwall Walk. (See Floodwall Walk in the PLACES section of this book.)

Floodwall Park — At the intersection of Hull and 2nd Street, directly across the street from the Richmond Railway Museum, there is a 15-car parking lot. (See Floodwall Walk in the PLACES section of this book.)

I-95 Bridge — Brander Street passes beneath the I-95 Bridge beneath which, on both sides of the street, is space to park dozens of cars. This area has access to fishing as well as the Slave Trail (leading upstream onto the Floodwall and downstream to Ancarrow's Landing).

Brander Street Roadside — On the north side of Brander Street, just downstream from the I-95 Bridge, is a streetside parking area that will accommodate 10 cars. It offers a wooded pathway that quickly connects with the Slave Trail which goes both upstream and downstream.

Ancarrow's Landing — Follow Maury Street to its northern end and you'll arrive at Brander Street. Turn right and in just over a half mile you'll arrive at Ancarrow's Landing and its humongous parking lot (~200 cars). (See Ancarrow's Landing in the PLACES section of this book.)

North Side (listed from east to west):

▲ PICTURED ABOVE:
Alyx Staruk, who works with the nonprofit organization Vegan Action, is seen here at the 2022 VA Pridefest on Brown's Island.

Rocketts Landing Residential Community — Located at 4708 Old Main Street, there is some street parking (~20 cars) along Old Main Street and scattered additional street parking elsewhere in the complex. (See Rocketts Landing Residential Community in the PLACES section of this book.)

Rocketts Landing Wharf — Turn towards the river where Nichols meets East Main and you'll be on Wharf Street that provides access to a spacious parking area (~50 cars) beside the river. (See Rocketts Landing Wharf in the PLACES section of this book.)

Great Shiplock Park — Located at the intersection of Dock and Pear Streets, Great Shiplock Park has a 25-car parking lot that is always full on weekends and at other busy times. Just across Dock Street from the Park is a small gravel area that can accommodate approximately 10 cars. And there is street parking for a few more cars on Pear Street. But be careful crossing Dock Street on foot; there is continual traffic, often going over the speed limit. (See Great Shiplock Park and Chapel Island in the PLACES section of this book.)

Dock Street — There are several pay-to-park lots along Dock Street east of its intersection with 14th Street. This area offers immediate access to the Canal Walk and the beginning of the Virginia Capital Trail.

14th Street Takeout — There is room for approximately 20 cars in this lot that is designated for vehicles carrying kayaks, canoes, etc. Its address, 1601 East Byrd Street, is a bit misleading. If you're headed south towards the river on 14th Street, turn left immediately after you pass the Floodwall. (It's common to miss the turn unless you know it's there.) Caution: When departing this area, be careful. There is usually plenty of traffic and it's difficult to see what's coming. (See 14th Street Takeout in the PLACES section of this book.)

Passport Parking — This is a huge pay-to-park lot (100+ cars) adjacent to the 14th Street Takeout. It's necessary to have the payment app on your mobile device.

Virginia Street — On Virginia Street, south of East Canal Street, there is street parking for 7 cars. If you're fortunate enough to get one of these, you're within a few steps of the Canal Walk.

East Canal Street — There is street parking for approximately 12 cars on the north side of East Canal Street's block immediately west of its intersection with Virginia Street.

1200 East Byrd Street — Go east on Byrd Street, but as Byrd converges left onto 12th Street, swerve right instead (but don't turn right into the Pipeline Overlook area) and you'll see a giant parking area straight ahead bordered by the Flood Wall on the right. Even though you'll see some Private Parking signs that imply that all of the spaces are for residents of The Locks Apartments, the numbered spaces along the Flood Wall as well as the 20 paystation spaces along the fence are available to the general public.

Pipeline Overlook — Go east on Byrd Street until it turns left into 12th Street, but turn RIGHT instead and then make an immediate left behind the Floodwall and you'll arrive at a tiny parking area (8 cars?) that provides access to a path down to the river and another path east to the stairway to climb down onto the Pipeline. (See Pipeline in the PLACES section of this book.)

East Byrd Street — On East Byrd Street between 11th and 12th Streets are diagonal back-in parking spaces for 16 cars. (Easy walk to the Pipeline Overlook, etc.)

South Second Street — There is available street parking (~25 cars) on South Second Street near its intersection with Brown's Island Way. From there you can walk downhill to access the footbridge to Belle Isle as well as the American Civil War Museum, Brown's Island, and the Canal Walk.

▲ PICTURED ABOVE: Noah Kelly (20) and Cinnamon (4) are travelers who were last in New York and will soon depart for California. Noah, currently saving money to buy a school bus, is a craftsman: formerly tie-dyed shirts, and forthcoming walking sticks.

Belle Isle Footbridge — Near the western end of Tredegar Street there is a parking lot for approximately 60 cars. This is the closest parking area to the Belle Isle Footbridge and it fills quickly! (See Belle Isle in the PLACES section of this book.)

South 5th Street — On South 5th Street, between East Byrd and Tredegar Streets, is street parking for approximately 50 cars. Walk from there downhill to Tredegar Beach, Brown's Island, the Belle Isle Footbridge, the Canal Walk, T. Tyler Potterfield Memorial Bridge, etc.

North Bank Park, aka Texas Beach — This section of the James River Park System is at the end of Texas Avenue and the parking lot has room for around 50 cars. There is additional street parking available on nearby neighborhood streets. But everything fills up quickly on weekends. (See North Bank Park in the PLACES section of this book.)

North Bank Trailhead — This is a 30-car lot that you can't miss on Pump House Drive and is located at the trailhead of the North Bank Trail. If the lot happens to be full, there is lots of parking (~100 cars) on Pump House Drive.

Pump House Park — This area of the James River Park System is readily recognized on Pump House Drive and offers generous (100 cars?) street parking. Even on weekends you can usually find parking spaces. (See Pump House Park in the PLACES section of this book.) ≈

Today's River Conditions (Now As You Read This)

HowsTheJamesRVA – Ryan Abrahamsen of Richmond tech company Terrain360 partnered with Riverside Outfitters and Friends of James River Park to create a three-times-daily look at the urban river's water level, water temperature, air temperature, and weather forecast via a Twitter and Instagram feed entitled HowsTheJamesRVA which is easily accessed on mobile devices.

Companies & Organizations

Of course you can find information and videos and maps regarding almost anything regarding Richmond's James River on the Internet via Google, YouTube, etc., including opportunities for classes, instruction, camps, outings, information, volunteerism, advocacy, and on and on. Following is a list of some of the companies, organizations, and websites that have special relationships with the James River. Simply browsing the websites will no doubt make you aware of lots of things that you likely would have never thought of. And DO put yourself on their mailing lists! (If you know of companies/organizations that I should have included, e-mail me at jbryanfish@aol.com.)

Richmonder Max Kadunce, seen here on Brown's Island at the VA Pridefest, is a trumpet player and a Kinetic Imaging major at VCU.

AllTrails (Alltrails.com) — The site has nice maps and descriptions of trails along the James and provides helpful info regarding dogs, bird watching, kids, views, wildflowers, etc. From the intro comments about the North Bank Buttermilk Trail Loop: "Get to know this 6.2-mile loop trail near Richmond, Virginia. Generally considered a moderately challenging route, it takes an average of 2 h 14 min to complete. This is a very popular area for birding, hiking, and mountain biking, so you'll likely encounter other people while exploring. The trail is open year-round and is beautiful to visit anytime. Dogs are welcome."

American Civil War Museum (acwm.org) — Located along the James River at 480 Tredegar Street, the Museum is on the site of the historic Tredegar Ironworks that opened in 1837. It was the largest facility of its kind in the South and produced a variety of products including steam locomotives. It became the major producer of artillery for the South in the Civil War. The Museum's public parking lot (not free) offers easy-walk access to Brown's Island, the T-Pott Bridge, and the Footbridge to Belle Isle.

▲ PICTURED ABOVE: Parker Ross is a sales rep for Appomattox River Company (paddleva.com) — the go-to and largest paddling supply dealer on the East Coast.

Appomattox River Company (Facebook and paddleva.com) — This long-time RVA-trusted company no longer has a site in the Richmond area, but continues to be valued as an important vendor of paddle-craft and equipment.

Beyond Boundaries (beyondboundariesrva.org) — "Specializes in guiding participants with disabilities, veterans, at-risk youth, and recovery programs on outdoor adventures" — many of which are on the urban James.

Blue Sky Fund (blueskyfund.org) — This organization "provides transformational experiences for urban youth through outdoor education" and skills ranging from rock climbing to kayaking, much of which takes place along Richmond's James River.

Capital Trees (capitaltrees.org) — "Together with private citizens and public benefactors, Capital Trees works to make Richmond a greener, more livable city by creating public landscapes that foster community building, environmental stability, economic investment and healthier lifestyles." Most notable is the organization's wonderful work along the river, especially the Low Line and Great Shiplock Park.

Dancer Christy Siller, from Florida where she was a member of the Sarasota Ballet, works on a sunprinting artwork along the Low Line. She also enjoys Texas Beach, Pump House Park, and the Pipeline.

Coastal Canoeists (coastals.org) — "Coastals is a family-oriented club dedicated to the enjoyment and advancement of paddlesports and consists of canoeists, kayakers and others from the southeastern U.S., but primarily from Virginia. Activities of the club include an active club volunteer-coordinated trip roster with trips for members, at all skill levels, happening nearly every weekend of the year." The website has an extensive and comprehensive section on safety – highly recommended for all paddle-craft.

ConnectVA (Connectva.org) — This website, provided by The Community Foundation, gives info about events and opportunities, including those relating to the James River, provided by nonprofit organizations such as Friends of James River Park.

Crosswind Paddle Company (crosswindpaddle.com) — Focusing on the flatwater portion of the James River upstream from Richmond at Robious Landing, this company sells, rents, and provides instruction and events for standup paddleboarding.

Cycling Virginia (cyclingvirginia.com) — "Your one stop resource for information on cycling in the Commonwealth of Virginia. This website was developed to consolidate and showcase the diversity of cycling in Virginia and make it easier to find what you're looking for. No more searching through a multitude of websites or Facebook pages to find Virginia cycling clubs, activities and events held throughout the year."

eBird (ebird.org) — "eBird is among the world's largest biodiversity-related science projects, with more than 100 million bird sightings contributed annually by eBirders around the world and an average participation growth rate of approximately 20% year over year. A collaborative enterprise with hundreds of partner organizations, thousands of regional experts, and hundreds of thousands of users, eBird is managed by the Cornell Lab of Ornithology." On this website you can find very specific locations and sightings as well as comprehensive info on all things birding.

The Feminist Bird Club, Richmond, VA Chapter (Instagram @fbc.rva) — Co-founded by Dylan Slusarz in 2022, the Club's "mission is to make birding and the outdoors inclusive and affirming to people who may not have safe access to it, and leverage people's passion for the environment and social justice to help create lasting social change." Many of the outings take place in James River Park.

Friends of James River Park (jamesriverpark.org) — This is THE organization to know about, to be involved with, and to join. The website is robust with information about every aspect of James River Park: sites, activities, history, flora and fauna, trails, safety, etc. etc. etc. And there are wonderful photos, maps, and videos; information for teachers; and an events calendar. Spend time on this website and you will be rewarded!

Josh Stutz, Executive Director of Friends of James River Park along with board member Jean Linnell who works at a VCU student center.

▲ PICTURED ABOVE: Charleston, WV native Penn Markham, an electrical engineer for Dominion Energy, and President of Friends of Pump House, moved to Richmond from Knoxville. He loves Richmond, especially the city's variety of historic architecture.

Friends of Pump House (friendsofpumphouse.org) — "Friends of Pump House is a volunteer-led non-profit organization dedicated to preserving, protecting, and restoring the historic Byrd Park Pump House. Our members devote their time and energy to this cause in a variety of ways, including participation in monthly workdays, hosting tours and educational events, advocacy, historic research, and fundraising."

Hike It Baby (trails.hikeitbaby.com) — "Hike it Baby Family Trail Guide is an online resource to help families with children source trails that little legs can hike and parents can feel comfortable with. Hike details are sourced and have been hiked by families who participate in our community." There is great information about the trails along the James River in Richmond.

James River Association (thejamesriver.org) — Although the James River Association embraces the entire length of the James River, it is headquartered in Richmond and thus has a special affinity for the Richmond portion of the river. Following is from the website's introductory statements: "The mission of the James River Association is to be a guardian of the James River. We provide a voice for the river and take action to promote conservation and responsible stewardship of its natural resources. JRA monitors the river, responds to problems, seeks policy changes, and implements on-the-ground projects to restore the river's health. We protect through our Watershed Restoration, James Riverkeeper, and River Advocacy programs. JRA helps communities benefit from the river by increasing river access, supporting river-related events, and implementing volunteer projects. We connect through

our Environmental Education and Community Conservation programs."

The website is loaded with information and opportunities of value for persons who enjoy the Richmond portion of the river: events such as "Paddle Through History — The Fall Line of the James;" how-to information such as how to build a rain barrel for your home; webinars such as "The Great Return of the Atlantic Sturgeon;" virtual classrooms for school-age children with topics such as "Fish of the James River," "Make a Rain Gauge," and "360 Degree Scavenger Hunt;" the biannual "State of the James" report; and how to become an official RiverRat, volunteers who patrol the river and report their sightings. Also, through a partnership with Terrain360 (terrain360.com), the website enables viewers to explore the entire river via high-res, 360-degree panoramic images: "Take a tour of the James, scout out boat landings and plan your paddle trip from the comfort of your desktop." Be sure to be aware of the website's "Stay Safe on the James" section!

And finally, the website links to "James River Watch" that allows you to click on a specific part of the river (Pony Pasture, Huguenot Flatwater, etc.) and see the river level and flow, water and air temperatures, E Coli concentration, and turbidity.

James River Hikers — A Meetup and Facebook group, here's the group's welcome message: "Organized to explore some of Richmond's most little known beautiful nature and history, get exercise with challenging hikes and meet a diverse group of locals that may become your new friends. We will walk the trails by James River and to historical areas all over Richmond."

James River Women (Facebook) — Lots of outings on the river. "We are dedicated to supporting and promoting the inclusion of lady and femme-identifying paddlers within the whitewater paddling community."

JRAC — James River Advisory Council (jrac-va.org) — "The James River Advisory Council provides a forum for the diverse interests along the James River in Central Virginia and engages the public about issues and challenges facing the river. JRAC's vision is a healthy, beautiful, economically vital and accessible James River that is cared for by a diverse and engaged community that acts on its behalf. JRAC's membership includes representatives from local jurisdictions, businesses and industry, civic organizations and individuals. By leading discussions about the river, and hosting regional events and programs, the council sets the tone for positive and interactive relationships among partners throughout the region." JRAC's signature events include the annual James River Week, and James River Regional Cleanup.

▲ PICTURED ABOVE: Matt Rosenberg heads James River Outdoor Coalition.

JROC — James River Outdoor Coalition (jroc.net) — "James River Outdoor Coalition (JROC) is a non-profit organization that supports the James River Park System through donations and volunteer efforts to improve park facilities. JROC also takes an active role in issues that affect the Park System's usage and its natural resources." One example of JROC's highly beneficial projects is the construction of the universal access ramp at Huguenot Flatwater. Becoming involved with JROC is one of the best ways to take an active role in helping to maintain the river's vitality. How do you get started? Easy, just attend one of JROC's monthly meetings; the schedule is on the website, and anyone can attend. No RSVP required; just show up.

Maymont (maymont.org) — Located at 1000 Westover Road, and with the Kanawha Canal and James River on its southern boundary (but no access), Maymont is a family-friendly, historic estate and park with gardens, native wildlife, historic mansion, and its Robins Nature Center that invites you to "Dive

in for an immersive James River experience including native river wildlife, interactive animations, digital touch pools, lively recreation ... Fun for all ages!"

MORE (The Mid-Atlantic Off-Road Enthusiasts (more-mtb.org) — "MORE's Mission is to build an inclusive grass roots mountain biking community and organization with the express purpose of expanding riding opportunities and increasing trail access throughout the Mid-Atlantic region. This is to be achieved by building and maintaining multi-use sustainable trails through promoting volunteerism, partnerships and educational outreach across user groups, thereby enabling fun and rewarding riding experiences for all ages and ability levels."

Paddling.com — Not a Richmond-specific company or website, but it has some good info about paddling. It's hard to search for specific paddling locations, such as Richmond's Pipeline. But if you do find a specific area, the comments can be very helpful. For example, for Huguenot Flatwater, one of the comments pointed out that if you go downstream you soon encounter dangerous rapids and hydraulics.

Peak Experiences / Passages Adventure Camp (peakexperiences.com) — Headquartered at 1375 Overbrook Road, Peak Experiences boasts "Richmond VA's Premiere Rock Climbing Facilities." Its well-known and extremely popular connection to the river is its Passages Adventure Camp that provides a variety of experiences for ages 5-17: climbing, kayaking, biking and more! The website offers eye-widening photos and videos and information. (Check out the video for "The Blast!")

Kevin Tobin is the owner of Peak Experiences which includes Passages Adventure Camps.

Richmond Audubon Society (richmondaudubon.org) — "Richmond Audubon Society (RAS) is a chapter of the National Audubon Society and is dedicated to the observation and conservation of birds and other wildlife. Our members participate in local conservation efforts, habitat restoration, and monitoring of applicable legislation. We have over 1,400 members throughout Central Virginia, made up of a diverse group of people from various backgrounds, interests and birding experience levels. Come join us for some bird watching, fellowship, advocacy and fun!" Highly relevant to this guidebook is that this organization's members conduct a bird count each January in the James River Park System.

Richmond BridgePark Foundation (bridgeparkrva.com) — "BridgePark is a proposed linear public park that would span the James River and connect the riverfront experience to the City Center, on both sides of the James. The park would transform 9th Street (including a portion of the Manchester Bridge over the beautiful James River) into a world-class destination for biking, walking, art, education, events, and community engagement."

Richmond Community Rowing richmondcommunityrowing.com — See ROWING section of this book.

Richmond Cycling Corps (richmondcyclingcorps.org) — Richmond Cycling Corps uses cycling as a vehicle "to educate and empower the lives of Richmond youth," mostly living in the public housing projects in Richmond's East End. The cycling includes trails along the river and James River Park, and the organization operates "Kickstand," a bike rental facility at 3011 Water Street.

Richmond Railroad Museum (richmondrailroadmuseum.com) — Located at 102 Hull Street, just a short block from the Floodwall Walk, and open 11-4 on Saturdays and 1-4 on Sundays, the Richmond Railroad Museum exhibits historic railroading materials and equipment, track car, baggage car, caboose, Richmond's largest HO scale model railroad, and much more.

Richmond Road Runners Club (rrrc.org) — This is the club for runners in the Richmond region, and is the go-to source and organizer for races, teams, and events. The Club has contributed significant funding and volunteer work for trails throughout the James River Park. The Spring 2022 issue of its online magazine, *MILES & MINUTES*, featured a wonderfully comprehensive article about the James River Park System.

Richmond Tourism (visitrichmondva.com) — This website contains information and links for enjoying the entire city, including things associated with the river, such as Belle Isle, Canal Boat Cruises, Dominion Energy Riverrock, James River Park System, and on and on. There are very helpful sections with titles such as "Family Friendly," "Outdoors," "Trails," "This Weekend," and "Events." AND you can get them to send you a free Visitor's Guide "chock-full-of-info book on greater RVA."

Be sure to sign up for the newsletter/e-list: "updates about events, festivals, attractions, food, craft beer and special promotions," some of which involve the James River.

River City Crew (rivercitycrew.org) — See ROWING section of this book.

Riverside Outfitters (riverside-outfitters.com) — This long-time admired company offers just about everything, for just about every age, that involves Richmond's James River: rentals, trips, camps, etc.; rock climbing, tree-climbing, biking, kayaking, tubing, etc. The website is robust with offerings, photos and videos. (One caution — it's common for youth activities to fill quickly.)

▲ PICTURED ABOVE: Riverside Outfitters President Matt Perry and Guided Boating Director Jen Jimenez.

RVAHUB (Rvahub.com) — Search "James River" on this site and you'll find all sorts of current info regarding the Richmond section of the river such as: *Men's Journal* naming the James River Park Loop one of the best running trails in America, Regional Clean Up Day on the James, the James River Association's "Kids in Kayaks" program, and more.

▲ PICTURED ABOVE: Jas Johnson (left) who works for Capital One, and Taila Fleming who works for MAC Cosmetics, enjoy all of James River Park and the river, including the 2022 VA Pridefest.

rvaMORE (rvamore.org) — "rvaMORE is a diverse group of trail enthusiasts with a passion for advocating for access to great trails in the Richmond Region. We are mountain bikers, runners, boaters, hikers and nature lovers with a commitment to our parks and to all those who find enjoyment there. Our work is supported through membership, donations, corporate sponsorship, and volunteer efforts." The organization develops, maintains, funds, and provides educational programs for trails. Events include social bike rides and trail work. The website includes detailed trail descriptions, maps, instructive videos, and extras such as guidance on "Trail Building Basics" and International Mountain Bicycling Association's "Rules of the Trail."

RVAPaddlesports (rvapaddlesports.com) — This company annually serves thousands of customers of all ages for outings, rentals, and classes in kayaking, canoeing, paddleboarding, rafting, climbing, and more — lots of exciting photos and details on the website. Special

Patrick Griffin,
Founder of
RVA Paddlesports

offerings include a July 4 Fireworks on the River outing, two-day courses for Sierra Rescue River Certification and Wilderness First Aid, and pop-up rafting opportunities (such as for the 2022 PrideFest).

Sierra Cub, Virginia Chapter, (sierraclub.org) — Headquartered in Richmond, this chapter and its Falls of the James Group often offers special opportunities related to the urban James River.

Sportable (sportable.org) — "Creates opportunities to make sports accessible for individuals with physical disabilities and visual impairments" — including opportunities in and on the urban James.

▲ PICTURED ABOVE: Josh Sloan, avid climber/biker/paddler prior to a spinal cord injury, learned to be active in the outdoors again via Sportable (sportable.org).

Sports Backers (sportsbackers.org) — This organization embraces a fundamental mission of "transforming greater Richmond into the most physically active community in the nation by leading the area in embracing and celebrating an active lifestyle." Some of the organization's most popular events are on and alongside the river, including the annual Dominion Energy Riverrock.

Vintage Tony Gilmore

SWIM GUIDE (theswimguide.org) — The site provides info about more than 8,000 swimming areas, including maps, descriptions, and water quality information about some of the swimming areas along Richmond's James River. Here's the intro info about Pony Pasture: "Pony Pasture Park is a great section of the James for multiple water recreation purposes. There are multiple shaded walking trails with some little-known swimming areas. Pony Pasture has a boat ramp for paddlers to access the class 1 and 2 rapids, but swimming at the ramp is not permitted. There are bathrooms and a large parking lot."

Tandem Kayak Adventures (tandemkayakadventures.com) — This Richmond company offers kayak outings, mostly on the urban James. "Book a guided kayak tour with us! We specialize in gorgeous routes that are 100% Flatwater. The calmness means you get to look around and take in the surroundings as you and a friend glide on top of the water. Our kayaks are stable, extremely comfortable, easy-to-use, and our guides will take you to the best spots this area has to offer!"

Terrain360 (Terrain360.com) — Terrain360's website enables viewers to explore the entire river via high-res, 360-degree panoramic images. This allows you to virtually scout the river and plan your outing. You can view and tour specific sections such as Huguenot Flatwater to Reedy Creek, Pony Pasture to Reedy Creek, Belle Isle Water, and even Williams Island.

Trail Hut (thetrailhut.com) — Here you can find all sorts of climbing and hiking gear for purchase or rental – much of it on consignment. The website contains nicely detailed maps of the 6.5-mile James River Loop trail, the 1.1-mile Buttermilk and Reedy Creek Trail Loop, the 3-mile Forest Hill Park Loop trail, and the 2.2-mile Pipeline Trail and Floodwall Loop.

▲ PICTURED ABOVE: Friends Sydney Owens (Virginia Tech student majoring in nutrition/exercise), Bella Richey (ODU majoring in business administration), and Katryn Combs (ODU, nursing) grew up in Richmond and enjoy the river's rocks and rapids.

Venture Richmond (venturerichmond.com) — Venture Richmond, whose mission is to enhance the vitality of downtown Richmond, has a wonderful website. It has a grand abundance of information and links regarding the urban James River and its history, activities, and access: canal cruises, downtown parking and transportation, 22 miles of trails, riverside events such as the Richmond Folk Festival and Dominion Energy Riverrock, Belle Isle, history medallions along the Canal Walk, public art and statues, and much more.

Virginia Boat Club (Facebook) — With its boats and dock at the upstream end of Rocketts Landing (4708 Old Main Street), the Virginia Boat Club "is a not-for-profit organization with the mission of promoting rowing in Greater Richmond, VA area. The VBC offers members the opportunity to enjoy miles of scenic recreational and competitive rowing on the James River." The Club offers instruction, competition, and recreation for adults 18 and older.

Virginia Capital Trail Foundation (virginiacapitaltrail.org) — "The Virginia Capital Trail is a 51.7-mile, fully-paved trail that runs through 4 jurisdictions (City of Richmond, Henrico County, Charles City County, and James City County) with dozens of attractions along the way." Its western head is in downtown Richmond where 17th Street meets the Floodwall, and goes east for 1.3 miles within the city limits along the Canal and the James River before proceeding east.

Virginia Commonwealth University Outdoor Adventure Program (recsports.vcu.edu) — This program is open not only to VCU students but also to community members. It features equipment rentals (e.g. canoes), expertise, and outings (e.g. whitewater rafting, flatwater paddling).

Virginia Department of Wildlife Resources (dwr.virginia.gov) — This governmental entity has an extremely robust website on everything outdoors. Just search "James River" and you'll see many entries ranging from descriptions of the sections of James River Park, to the live Shad Cam at the Bosher's Dam Fishway (that includes videos of various species of fish swimming through the Fishway), reports of bird species sightings at specific areas (such as The Wetlands) along the river, paddling skills, how and where to fish, and on and on. Exploring the website is an exciting adventure on its own.

Virginia Outside (virginiaoutside.com) — This youth-focused company offers summer camps and after-school programs on fishing, hiking, kayaking, mountain biking, rock climbing, etc. — much of which is located along the James River in Richmond.

◄ PICTURED LEFT: Kevin Dougherty (blue shirt and first aid kit) of Virginia Outside and mountain biking camp participants Trinity, Graham, Carson, Luke, Hank, Eddie, James, Ryan, Owen, Ethan, Jude, and Sean, taking a break at the Reedy Creek entrance to James River Park. Kevin moved from California to RVA three years ago with the intent to stay two years. Now he plans to never leave.

Waterfront RVA (www. waterfrontrva.com) — This is a walkup kayak and paddleboard rental company located right on the river at 415 Tredegar Street. They have everything you need, including basic instruction to paddle in this flatwater section of the urban James. (Good Facebook site with information, photos, videos.) ≈

▲ PICTURED ABOVE: Luis Castaneda and Preston Slaughter are guides with Waterfront RVA which provides walk-up kayak and paddleboard rentals and instruction, whitewater trips, and paddleboard yoga at the Tredegar Street put-in. www.waterfrontrva.com

Wisdom of Ralph White

RVA is fortunate to have engaged Ralph White as the first and long-time Manager of the James River Park System. His work received national attention and in 2006 he flew to San Francisco to receive the Sierra Club's national Distinguished Service Award. Ralph generously provided information, writings, advice, and wisdom for my 1997 guidebook, *The James River in Richmond — Your Guide to Enjoying America's Best Urban Waterway.*

When I interviewed him while compiling this new guidebook, I found that his passion for the James River Park System is, hard as it seems, even more fierce than when he was on the front line. Ralph's vision for James River Park continues to be big and broad and multi-faceted. He has a long list of recommendations: "a poetry guide rather than cops," "summer workers not just doing low-grade labor, but who are professionals in training and who have broad dreams about changing the world via nature," "citizen input and control," "walk-only trails (no bikes) for birders, etc.," "allowance for youthful exuberance (e.g. topless sunbathing)," and on and on.

One of Ralph's declarations is not only plaque-worthy, but might also be words to live by as all of us attend to the welfare of RVA's James River Park System: "I'm into the 'Let's all groove on nature' kind of thing."

Real estate attorney Carly and son Levin Nino enjoy biking on riverside trails — seen here beneath the Manchester Bridge.

Books

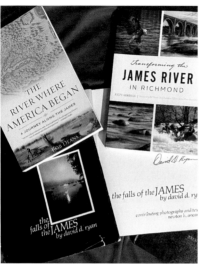

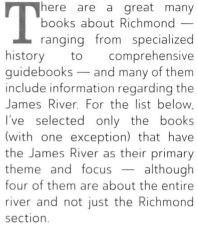

There are a great many books about Richmond — ranging from specialized history to comprehensive guidebooks — and many of them include information regarding the James River. For the list below, I've selected only the books (with one exception) that have the James River as their primary theme and focus — although four of them are about the entire river and not just the Richmond section.

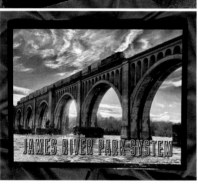

***A PHOTOGRAPHIC JOURNEY THROUGH THE JAMES RIVER PARK SYSTEM*, 2021, Bill Draper** — This beautiful book of photographs by Bill Draper presents "diverse views of the Park and the Richmond skyline captured on and off the beaten path in all four seasons." Bill has donated proceeds from sales (thousands and thousands of dollars) to Friends of James River Park.

***CABELL'S CANAL: THE STORY OF THE JAMES RIVER AND KANAWHA*, 2000, Langhorne Gibson** — *Cabell's Canal* covers river improvements on the James River in the Commonwealth of Virginia from Colonial times through the demise of the James River and Kanawha Company in 1880.

***FALLS OF THE JAMES ATLAS*, 1995, W.E. Trout III, James Moore III, George D. Rawls** — Although the book's primary purpose is to describe and give information about the history of the river's structures, it is full of other information. Its map alone will be of great interest to anyone who has an interest in the history of the urban James River.

IN RIVER TIME: THE WAY OF THE JAMES, **1985, Ann Woodlief** — The author guides us along the James' twisting paths, shows us its history and geography and sociology, stops at every significant marker buoy from Pocahontas to Kepone, and pauses to wet our toes and scent our nostrils and muddy our fingers: philosophy, metaphysics, heart and soul.

JAMES RIVER GUIDE: INSIDERS' PADDLING AND FISHING TRIPS FROM HEADWATERS DOWN TO RICHMOND, **2014, Bruce Ingram** — This book covers the river from its headwaters to Richmond and has great information on the river's history and of course paddling and fishing — including a variety of maps.

MCELLIGOT'S POOL, **Dr. Seuss, 1947** — This one's not literally about the James River, but it's my favorite Dr. Seuss book. Its primary theme is that even a taken-for-granted waterhole can, like our urban James River, hold marvelous and unending surprises. (The book is now out of print due to the Dr. Seuss Foundation's realization that a word used in the book — Eskimo — has a racist and hurtful history.)

RIVERFRONT RENAISSANCE, **2016, Brenton S. Halsey** — John W. Bates, III summed it up in the book's Foreword: "It is the story of Richmond's riverfront, written by Brent Halsey, the man who not only intimately knows and loves the James River and its history, but is personally responsible, more than anyone else, for the revitalization of Richmond's riverfront."

THE CANAL ON THE JAMES, **2009, T. Gibson Hobbs** — From the book's front pages: "Over a period of thirty years T. Gibson Hobbs collected every scrap of information he could find about the James River and Kanawha Canal in Virginia. This book is a compilation of his research — the talks he gave, the slides he showed, and the maps on which he meticulously cataloged the works of the canal system."

THE FALLS OF THE JAMES, **1975, David D. Ryan** — A revered classic, this is the book that put a public spotlight on the urban river's non-industrial glory: its waters and recreation, its history, its flora and fauna, its poetry. The book of course chronicles the river's history and development, but it also encourages a heartfelt appreciation of the river for its even greater value. It concludes with this: "A person who takes the time and effort to understand, to respect, and to love this river will be rewarded a thousand times more than he or she can give in return."

▲ PICTURED ABOVE: This is the first visit to Belle Isle for Sudip Manandhar and Ginni Bajracharya, both engineers, who moved to Richmond a year ago from Fort Worth. They say they like RVA better than TX – especially because of access to the wild outdoors in the middle of the city

THE JAMES RIVER, 2015, William A. Fox — "With more than 200 images, *The James River* seeks to raise awareness about this great river and its history while helping to protect and preserve it for the future."

THE JAMES RIVER IN RICHMOND — YOUR GUIDE TO ENJOYING AMERICA'S BEST URBAN WATERWAY, 1997, John Bryan - Now out of print, I published this 326-pager just prior to the real blossoming of the information age: computers, websites, mobile phones, e-mail, Facebook, and on and on. While some of its information is now outdated, there is much that continues to be both interesting and relevant.

THE RIVER WHERE AMERICA BEGAN, 2007, Bob Deans — Bob Deans' Introduction concludes with this: "... it is from this majestic river, along the muddy banks of the James, that our country got its start four centuries ago. It was into these waters we first waded — red, white, and black – and from them emerged as one. It is here, in that sense, our national story begins." Beautifully written, rich in thoughtfully examined history, and compelling throughout, this book is not only educational, but also an engaging read.

TRANSFORMING THE JAMES RIVER IN RICHMOND, 2020, Ralph Hambrick — I hope nobody who wants to learn about the James River in Richmond has to be limited to only one book, but if so, this one would be my choice. From history to high waters, from kayaking to climbing, from politics to people, Ralph Hambrick has put together a great gathering of virtually all of the things to know and consider about our river. ≈

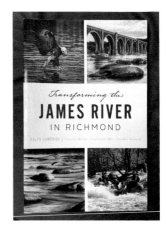

Emancipation & Freedom Monument

By Fred P. Orelove

As a white man not originally from Richmond, I am keenly aware that the monument represents a history and experience that is not my own. Yet each time I return to the monument, situated at the entrance to Brown's Island, I find myself moved by the words and, especially, by the images.

▼ PICTURED BELOW: Fred Orelove overlooking the river at the Richmond Folk Festival.

The monument grew out of the Virginia Dr. Martin Luther King, Jr. Memorial Commission's commemoration of the 150th anniversary of the Emancipation Proclamation and the abolition of slavery in the United States. Designed by Thomas Jay Warren, the monument features two 12-foot bronze statues, representing a man, woman, and infant newly freed from slavery.

Shockoe Bottom, to the immediate east, was the center of Richmond's slave trade, and its proximity to the James River is no accident. The slave-trade auction houses and slave jails have long been razed and paved over. But the effects of that period continue to reverberate.

The woman in the monument is standing on a pedestal, with the word "FREEDOM" etched on one side. She is facing south, towards the river that perhaps carried her and her ancestors to that spot. Her baby is cradled in her left arm, and her right arm holds aloft a document with the date the Emancipation Proclamation took effect, January 1, 1863.

The man stands facing north, his bare

back depicting the scars of lashes. The manacles, standing suspended in space, have dropped from his outstretched arms. His eyes are closed as if in silent prayer.

Along the base of the monument are depicted ten individuals, five Virginians who fought against slavery (pre-Emancipation) and five who fought for equality (post-Emancipation). A brief biography is provided for each person. I was somewhat surprised and embarrassed that I was familiar with fewer than half of the individuals. To that end, this monument is not only inspirational and healing, but educational.

In his famous "I Have a Dream" speech, Dr. King, quoting from Scripture, declared "We will not be satisfied until justice rolls down like waters and righteousness like a mighty stream." The Emancipation and Freedom Monument will remind future generations what was lost and, especially, what was regained, thanks to the vision and leadership of courageous African American Virginians. ≈

VIRGINIANS WHO FOUGHT FOR EQUALITY

Andrew Knight with a James River shad.

Andrew Knight's Advice on Fishing at Ancarrow's Landing in April

See more from Andrew on Instagram: @rvajamesriverfishreport

In April this portion of the river is filled with spawning shad and stripers. Use a small gold, silver, or chartreuse spoon with a half-ounce egg sinker attached three feet above the spoon. Cast as far as you can and reel fast so that the spoon doesn't have a chance to reach the bottom and get hung. When you cast, cast UPstream; the current will bring your line back down. The farther upstream you can position yourself the better. Be mindful of the vines hanging from the rocks; your line can get hung in them. Be careful about reaching down to get the line, and use heavier line — at least 10-pound — so it has less chance of breaking. And finally, be friendly; in April there are lots of anglers and limited space. ≈

At the Bottom of the Canal

(Spring, 1996)

This one goes out to Tanya R. and to faraway lonely lovers everywhere.

The four of us — Thomas and I and Trevor and his dad Morrie — have a purpose: to scour the bottom of the newly dry entrance to the canal. To comb those first thousand yards in which boats hauled turn-of-the-century cargo. To encounter the maxim: The past is another country; people live differently there.

The city has pulled the plug on this all-important stretch of the canal — from Great Shiplock Park to the I-95 Bridge. The only water in it now is the few inches that creep in through the open lock every 12 hours with high tide. Supposedly there are a few years of repairs and renovations and reconstructions ahead as the city transforms the canal into an urban nicety.

But today it looks like what it is: an old, forgotten, trash- and debris-laden ditch — an urban ditch nestled between slivers of trees and bushes and undergrowth and overgrowth. We wear our mud shoes, we carry a metal detector to find treasures, and we carry a bucket to haul treasures.

Trevor, the youngest, gets first turn with the detector. It beeps immediately. Just a beer can. There are cans everywhere. It beeps immediately again — a rusted hunk of metal. There are rusted hunks of metal everywhere. Most are castoffs from the still-live train tracks that run along the length of the canal: spikes and

couplings and links of chain and other heavy-duty pieces. Thomas picks up one that's the shape and size of a crowbar. He'll carry it during our venture, using it to poke and dig.

Years ago I used to occasionally float my Jon boat in this canal and catch bass and bluegill. The water was always dark and murky and although my lures told me the canal's depth reached 10 feet, I had no way to visualize the configuration of the canal's floor. Now I see it. It's 10 feet deep near the lock and gradually shallows upstream towards the I-95 Bridge. Some of the shorelines still drop straight down. Others have caved in and now offer gentle slopes. The middle of the canal is wet from the high tide. Its mud still sinks fast: Thomas learns that as he tests a dark brown area that almost swallows his calf-high boot.

Fallen trees and overhanging bushes line the sides of the canal. There are occasional groups of pilings: tie-ups for canal boats. And the canal's current trophy is the 100-foot rusty metal boat that lists precariously along the opposite shoreline. "No," I tell Thomas and Trevor, "we can't go on the boat. First, there's no way to climb into it, and second, it would be too dangerous."

We walk along and kick among piles of debris hoping to find something of interest. We've turned off the detector; the abundance of metal has diffused its usefulness. There are plenty of bottles. I wish for bottle expertise. The only bottles I know are the old Coke bottles with cities on the bottoms. And I haven't found one of those in years.

"Trevor," I ask, "you know what I'd like to find?"

"What?"

"A fat wallet."

Trevor smiles and thinks. Then he looks up at me. "I'd like to find a gold coin."

"What would you do if we looked right over there next to that log and saw a gold coin on one side and a fat wallet on the other? Which would you choose if you got one and I got the other?"

"I'd take the gold coin," Trevor didn't hesitate, "because you wouldn't know what was in the fat wallet."

"But my fat wallet might contain a bunch of hundred-dollar bills."

"I don't care. I'd still take the gold coin."

We find neither. Our first unusual find will be a bad one.

"Mr. Bryan!" Trevor shouts from 100 feet up in front of me.

"Hey Dad!" Thomas joins him. "It's something dead!"

We determine it's a possum carcass. Not much left but skin and bones. A rotted remnant of aroma still lingers.

"Did he drown? "asks Trevor.

"I don't know," I reply. "Looks like he's been here a long time."

We move on without any young urges to poke it or kick it or turn it over.

"Hey Trevor!" We hear a distant shout.

"It's my dad," Trevor jubilantly exclaims as he points. "He's in the boat!"

Morrie is on the other side of the canal, and he has somehow scaled the 12-foot metal side of the old boat and is hailing us from atop its slanting deck.

"Hey you guys," he shouts. "This is really neat!"

"Can we go there?" Thomas and Trevor ask me in unison.

"Yeah, but there's no way to cross the canal here. We'll cross over when we get to the I-95 Bridge. Then we'll walk back along the other side.

"We'll be there later!" Trevor shouts. (He has a fine shouting voice.)

The canal floor has fewer treasures than I had expected. Mostly it's cans and bottles — new cans and bottles. I was hoping for castoffs from the previous century — maybe a cannonball or a rifle or a dish or a piece of silver. And I was anticipating contraband from the present century: handguns, bags of drug money, headless gangsters.

'Hey Dad!" Thomas shouts. "It's a CASH REGISTER!"

Sure enough, it appears that they are leveraging a cash register from the sandy mud. Maybe it's filled with money. Maybe old money: real silver, mercury dimes, buffalo nickels, wheat pennies, liberty half-dollars, Silver Certificates. I walk quickly to join them. Maybe the crooks couldn't get it open and had to toss it into the canal as the police got closer. They had to toss their bounty, toss the evidence. But we'll get it open. We'll use Thomas' crowbar if we have to. No cops chasing us today.

I arrive at the cash register and tilt it over. It's too heavy to lift. But it's not a cash register. It's some sort of electronic scale. It's the size of a cash register, and I guess it would appear to be a cash register to children searching for gold coins. But it's not a cash register. We walk on. The boys' next find will be even more provocative.

A single Kingfisher emits brief screams and alights on an overhanging branch a hundred yards ahead. I hear a Chickadee, too high to see, calling from one of the taller trees. The driftwood in this canal is awful; it doesn't have the swirling, gnarled character that you find on the main river. I pick up a seemingly old bottle every now and then and drop it into my bucket. I see continual stray pieces of metal. One looks like a discus; another round one with a hole is a huge washer.

There are shoes sprinkled in the canal. There are always abandoned shoes along rivers and oceans and creeks and canals. I see only sneakers today, maybe a total of 10. Only 2 match, and I see them 100 yards apart.

"Dad!" Thomas shouts. "We found a body!"

Thoughts stream through my head. Will I telephone the police immediately? Will this be the solution to a long-ago murder? Will there be a fat wallet next to the body?

As I walk closer I see a ribcage. It's a body alright. Thomas and Trever are standing back a couple of yards, unfamiliar with the rules for encountering a body. If there's a diamond ring on its finger, will I remove it? I find myself thinking about material things rather than having sympathy for the body's owner.

I arrive and look closely and see that the ribcage does appear to be human, but the tail isn't. Neither are the jaw and fangs. I turn to Thomas and Trevor. "It's a dog."

"Oh." They're disappointed. "Did he drown?"

I don't explain that not everything that ends up at the bottom of this canal necessarily drowned. We'll soon find another dead dog

that definitely did not drown.

Morrie appears from behind us and hustles to join us in time to see the dog bones. He marvels at how interesting the canal is and tells me he's going to add this to his list of places to regularly visit.

The next dog we find is different. It has decayed like the last one, but there is something different about the skeleton. There is no head. The boys don't notice this and I don't tell them. I've seen photos of headless dogs — photos of freshly decapitated dogs. The photos I've seen have been documentations of religious ceremonies — religions that worship dark deities. My friend Thomas Daniel took such photos for his "Jesus Saves" series. He has photographed all sorts of religious ceremonies — from tent revivals to snake handlings to dog sacrifices. The dog sacrifices are the most haunting. They're the photos I turn away from. They're the photos I decline to see more of. The poor dog we see now in this dry canal may have given his life in the name of a deity. I turn away and move on.

Thomas finds an old Coke bottle. "Look, Dad," he says as he holds it upside down and reads, "Cincinnati, Ohio." It goes into the bucket.

The religious dog is left behind us and true love is on the way.

We arrive at the I-95 Bridge and cross over to the other side of the canal and head back towards the boat. This side of the canal is next to Canal Street. Cars can pull over on the grass alongside the canal and easily dump things. We find an old washing machine, an old television, a sink, a toilet. "Someone must have been living down here!" Trevor concludes.

I lean over and pick up an old audio cassette tape. "Look, Trevor," I show him, "I bet this cassette has the instructions to buried treasure."

"Lemme see!" Trevor reaches and I hand him the cassette. It's dirty with dried mud.

"I bet the guy who buried the treasure in this canal recorded the instructions on how to find it on this cassette. I bet if we play the cassette we'll all be rich. I think we have just found a most amazing discovery."

Trevor's eyes are wide as he looks at the old cassette in his hands. Morrie stands behind him smiling and shaking his head. "That's right, Trevor," Morrie adds, "that cassette can show us the way to the treasure."

"I tell you what, Trevor," I lean closely. "You take that cassette home and put it in YOUR cassette player and listen carefully."

"Can we Dad?" he turns and asks Morrie.

We both smile and explain the joke to little Trevor.

"But it might have something good on it," he attempts to salvage some hope.

I explain that dirt and mud are not good for a tape player and we discard the tape and move on. But I won't discard the next cassette that we find.

"Hey Dad!" Thomas waves a bottled hand at me. "Enid, Oklahoma!" Another old Coke bottle. Enid was one of those cities that all of us heard of when we were kids. Enid's bottling plant must have shipped a lot of Cokes to Nashville. Thoughts about playing Coke bottle games come to me. The game of whose bottle came from farthest away was the most common. But my favorite was always the bluff game. You'd find a discarded bottle and then name three cities. The other person had to guess which one was on the bottle.

"Hey Dad!" Trevor shouts. "Here's a hubcap!" he shouts even louder.

"Trevor," Morrie says. "I can hear you without shouting. Let's try not to shout so loud."

"That's right, Trevor," I tease. "Out here in this canal we use our quiet voices. You should always save your shouting voice for the library."

Morrie laughs — thank goodness. "Yeah, Trevor, shout only in the library," he confirms.

"Trevor has a pretty healthy little shout there, doesn't he?" I say to Morrie.

"Geeeez!" is his reply as he stops smiling and shakes his head. "I can't stand it when he does it at home."

"When he's in your back yard we can always hear a Trevor shout at our house."

"I bet you can even hear him when he's indoors."

"I don't think so."

Trevor is listening to us and he responds with a very loud piercing scream, "HEYYYY, LISTEN TO THIIIIISSSS!!"

"Trevor!" Morrie doesn't smile.

"Hey Trevor," I get his attention. "If there were a screaming contest, would you enter?"

"I don't know."

"If there were a William Fox School Screaming Competition, do you think you'd want to enter?"

"He'd win," Morrie says.

"If we held a screaming competition at the Strawberry Street Festival," I look at Morrie, "do you think any kids could get their parents to pay a dollar for the entry fee?"

"I think every kid there would enter," he concludes.

"I think I'll do that." My wheels turn. "That'll be my volunteer job this year. I'll set up a table with a sign and the Festival will raise money from the screaming competition."

Morrie shakes his head.

"Who would be good judges?" I look at him.

"Not me," he responds without hesitation. "I won't be there."

"You don't want to watch Trevor win?"

"Nope."

"You think a lot of parents would leave during the competition?"

"Yep."

"Well, maybe it's not such a good idea then." Then I have an idea. "I know, the judges could wear those headsets that block out noise."

"That'd be good," Morrie nods.

"Hey Dad," Thomas gets my attention. "Listen to this," and emits an eerie, high-pitched scream that could curdle this canal water. Morrie winces and tilts his head.

"How do you do that, Thomas?" Morrie can't believe what he just heard.

"Like this," Thomas grins and does it again.

"How does he do that?" Morrie turns to me.

"Okay Thomas, that's enough," I say. "We'll enter you in the competition too."

We are almost to the boat when I see another cassette tape. This one is in its plastic case. There is a label. I pick it up to read the label, but everything has faded away. Except for an ink message that someone wrote on a piece of paper in the case: "Eric, I'll miss you this summer. I can't wait until next summer. All my love, Tanya."

True love. Young love. Tanya and Eric. True love forever. The tape is too dirty to play, and we'll never know what's on it. Probably the Righteous Brothers. "Unchained Melody." Or maybe Johnny Mathis. I show Morrie.

"Yeah," Morrie says as he hands the note back to me. "But look where we found the tape: at the bottom of this canal."

"You think Eric tossed it here?"

"Sure," Morrie nods and looks around. "Tanya gave him the tape, and as soon as she left town he tossed it. He was glad to be free of her."

"Holy Smokes!" I realize. "Eric was just waiting for summer so Tanya would leave. I bet he dropped her off at the bus station and drove by here and rolled down his window and just let it fly. 'Good riddance! Adios muchacha!' he probably said. Poor Tanya."

"Yeah, and then he drove on over to see his other little honey."

"His summer honey."

"Just tossed Tanya's tape into the canal — note and everything."

"Tanya probably wrote him every day all summer."

"And Eric probably tossed her letters without reading them."

"Tanya probably still thinks about him even after all these years."

"Her one true love. She's probably got a bunch of kids and a car pool and a dog or two, and late at night she still sometimes thinks about Eric."

"Secret lovers now — secret lovers separated by years and miles. That's what Tanya probably thinks."

"We ought to put an ad in the Personals."

"Yeah, 'Tanya, I still have the tape. Eric.'"

"Or, 'Tanya, no matter what anybody says, I didn't throw the tape into the canal. Eric.'"

We arrive at the old boat and Thomas and Trevor beg us to let them climb aboard. It takes some doing. Morrie finds foot- and hand-holds on the side of the boat and scales to the top and over the rail onto the deck. While I push from below, he pulls from above and we enable Thomas and Trevor to join him.

The boat is huge and old and rusty and metal and heavy. Not much left. This canal stopped being used 75 years ago, and I assume that's the age of the boat. There are only two sights of interest: the old bathroom — with toilet — and the old inscription engraved onto one of the interior walls: "Dead Annabel." I try to persuade Thomas and Trever that this is a ghost ship, but they don't bite. They're much more interested in the bathroom.

There is a rickety ladder down to a lower deck, but there is a foot of water at the bottom. Nothing to see down there either. The main source of fun is just standing on the boat and realizing that it's old. After a few minutes we climb out. Morrie and I marvel at the four-blade propeller that has a six-foot diameter.

Thomas and Trevor have discovered a dirt bike, a motorized dirt bike, a motocross-type bike. It's on its side at the bottom of the canal near the boat. They lift it and discuss the virtues of taking it home and cleaning it and riding it. Morrie and I of course squash their dreams. I'm not putting that nasty bike in my car.

It's past the time when I told JC we'd be back and we climb out of the canal and walk under the tracks towards the parking lot. Under the tracks are scattered pieces of coal. Amid the coal I find the final treasure of the day: a little white plastic packet, the size of a packet of ketchup and containing a product called "Grime-Free."

The front of the packet says it is "Waterless antiseptic skin cleaner." The back of the packet says it is "Tough on grime, gentle on skin. Quickly cleans most substances from most body areas." It contains ¼ ounce and was packed in Louisville.

I show it to Morrie and we both look up at the coal-dusted railroad track. "Can you imagine a big, burly railroad worker finishing a hard day of loading coal and then opening a dainty little packet of this stuff?"

"That's exactly what happened."

"Somehow I imagined those guys with big cakes of Lava sudsing down under an industrial shower somewhere."

"I guess not."

We drive home without having found a fat wallet or gold coin. My bucket now contains three Coke bottles — one of them a 10-ouncer —a handful of other bottles, Tanya's tape, and the packet of cleaner. Thomas wanted to take his "crowbar," but I made him leave it. You don't remove old metal objects from these historic lands and waters.

"Did you have fun?" Carol and JC greet us when we drive up.

"Hey Mom, listen to this!" Thomas and Trevor chime together. And they begin a screaming competition. ≈

WIN PRIZES PICKING UP LITTER

Richmond's James River "wilderness" does have its share of litter. We all know it's a good thing to pick up and dispose of litter, but some of us are just now learning about opportunities to earn prizes. The website is litterlotto.com, and the Instagram location is #BinItToWinIt. It's fun, the instructions are easy, and they'll know if you cheat.

James River Park System's Acreage Continues to Increase

Just as this book went to press it was announced that Josh and Carrie Belt Rogers had donated 3.46 acres of woodland property, which includes a third of a mile of the Buttermilk Trail, to the Capital Region Land Conservancy to be protected in perpetuity and to be added into the James River Park System. Carrie and Josh grew up in that neighborhood and developed their love of the outdoors there. "We are proud that this land will be conserved as parkland for all to enjoy for generations to come." PLUS, they are the owners/hosts of the Trailside Treehouse, a one-of-a-kind glamping destination that is just steps from the Buttermilk Trail and that Airbnb rates as one of the top 10 places to stay in Virginia. Visiting the website is an adventure in itself: trailsidetreehouse.com. ≈

Ralph White, longtime
Manager of the James
River Park System.

Accessible Adventures

by Shep Roeper, Director of Beyond Boundaries

Outdoor recreation has been on the rise in popularity for many years. If you journey back 150 years ago, in the late 1800s, we have the development of our first National Parks with Yosemite and Yellowstone, showing the country how important it is to protect and preserve our natural environment and historic spaces. The outdoor recreation field has come a long way since pioneers like Lawrence Holt and Kurt Hahn (Founders of Outward Bound, in the early 1940s) and Paul Petzoldt (Founder of NOLS, National Outdoor Leadership School, in the mid-1960s). These men were not only passionate about being outdoors, they knew how therapeutic and empowering being in nature is and wanted to educate others on how to recreate in a fun and safe way while also being good outdoor stewards.

With the rise in recreation, we also see the rise in outdoor education. Now you could not only 'play' in nature, but universities started to develop curriculums and programs so you could major in things like "Outdoor Recreation" and "Therapeutic Recreation," creating career opportunities. Radford University, where Beyond Boundaries' co-founders Shep Roeper and Kyle Burnette attended, is one of the leading outdoor recreation programs in the country. The skills and passion for the outdoors they developed in school would soon take them out to California for a while, and then back home, setting down roots again in Richmond.

Beyond Boundaries is a Richmond-based nonprofit that believes that adventure is for everyone (in fact, that is our motto/tagline). We also know that nature by itself is not always (rarely actually) accessible. It often takes a change in mindset, sometimes along with adaptive equipment, to make sure everyone can enjoy our natural spaces. Beyond Boundaries offers outdoor adventures to kids and adults with disabilities, at-risk youth, substance recovery programs, and veterans.

Richmond is lucky to be able to offer such a wide range of outdoor adventure opportunities like paddling, fishing, hiking, biking, rock climbing, and boating. All of these experiences can be done in and around the James River. Due to the diversity of our river, we spend most of our time white water rafting, kayaking, and fishing on the James River in Richmond. In the stretch of a few miles, you can find calm water that is great for beginner paddling and swimming, class IV white water for a more advanced experience, and diversity of fish species ranging from the migratory Shad to the Blue Catfish, a true river monster that can weigh up to 100 pounds!

You can see how special our river is, especially the diverse section we have in Richmond, which is a driving force for why we want to make sure everyone can enjoy it. With the hard work and support of local organizations, Richmond has accessible ramps at locations like Reedy Creek and Huguenot Flatwater, allowing more people to access the river. With new and innovative adaptive recreation gear being created around the world daily, Beyond Boundaries can better serve our participants and community. With a lengthy list of community partners and local outfitters, we can create more opportunities so that everyone living in or visiting Richmond can play outdoors, learn the skills to be a good environmental steward, and reap the many social, mental, and physical benefits outdoor recreation, and the James River specifically, provide! ≈

De izquierda a derecha en el Festival Que Pasa de RVA: Meta profesional R.J. Simmons y la propietaria de una pequeña empresa, Desiree Ramos, viven en Prince George. El ama de casa y nativo de RVA Marshall Jewett y su prometida Lee Maforah, una enfermera que se mudó a RVA hace 4 años desde Alabama, viven en Beaverdam. Todos disfrutan de todo el sistema de parques del río James.

Left to right at RVA's Que Pasa Festival: Meta professional R.J. Simmons and small business owner Desiree Ramos live in Prince George. Homemaker and RVA native Marshall Jewett and his fiancée Lee Maforah, a nurse who moved to RVA 4 years ago from Alabama, live in Beaverdam. They all enjoy the entire James River Park System.

Sección de Lengua Española

Ballet Latino de Virginia actuando en el James River Park de Richmond (de izquierda a derecha): Erin White, Maria Dolores Tuason, Jamie Allison LaNeave, Ana Ines King, Laren Davis. Foto de Tiffany Sunshine LaNeave.

Latin Ballet of Virginia performing in Richmond's James River Park (left to right): Erin White, Maria Delores Tuason, Jamie Allison LaNeave, Ana Ines King, Laren Davis. Photo by Tiffany Sunshine LaNeave.

Mensaje del Autor

Estoy tan complacido de que más y más miembros de nuestras comunidades de habla hispana estén disfrutando del río James de Richmond. Ofrezco tres sugerencias que pueden mejorar su disfrute.

1. Explore nuevos senderos, nuevas actividades y nuevos eventos.

2. Lleve a niños y amigos con usted.

3. Cuando tenga preguntas, acérquese a extraños y pregunte; El río urbano de Richmond saca a relucir la amabilidad, la amabilidad y la amabilidad en todos nosotros.

▲ **PICTURED ABOVE:** Reunión de quinceañeras en el puente T-Pott (de izquierda a derecha): Angi Rodriguez, Kelsy Kecinos, Rosa Raymundo Calo, Briana Fields, Alejandra J. Hidalgo Torres, Carlos Gallardo, Rudy Torcios, Justin Coronado, Eduardo Flores y Shatique Willis.

Quinceañera gathering on the T-Pott Bridge (left to right): Angi Rodriguez, Kelsy Kecinos, Rosa Raymundo Calo, Briana Fields, Alejandra J. Hidalgo Torres, Carlos Gallardo, Rudy Torcios, Justin Coronado, Eduardo Flores, and Shatique Willis.

Introducción
Por el senador estadounidense Tim Kaine

Me mudé de Kansas City a Richmond en 1984 para casarme con mi esposa Anne. Me llevó a Texas Beach a hacer un picnic cuando la visité por primera vez en el verano de 1982. Vimos nadadores y pescadores, garzas azules y navegantes, disfrutando del James. Era desierto justo en el corazón de la ciudad. Y mientras conducíamos por la ciudad, noté una proliferación inusual de canoas y kayaks en los techos de los automóviles. Me enganché.

En casi 40 años juntos, Anne y yo hemos centrado inconscientemente nuestra vida en James. Su familia nos regaló una canoa roja de Old Town para Navidad el primer año de nuestro matrimonio y tiene décadas de mellas y raspaduras de viajes frecuentes desde Pony Pasture hasta Reedy Creek. Caminamos y observamos aves en James River Park. Andamos en bicicleta a lo largo de Virginia Capital Trail. Hemos visto a nuestros tres hijos aprender a andar en canoa, kayak y escalar rocas en Belle Isle, primero como campistas y luego como consejeros. Hemos celebrado fiestas de cumpleaños y búsquedas del tesoro en los bancos. Asistimos a conciertos junto al río en Brown's Island y vimos fuegos artificiales reflejados en el agua de la marea cerca de Rocketts Landing. Nunca nos cansamos del James porque es diferente en cada estación y en cada nivel del agua. Y nosotros también.

Foto proporcionada por Tim Kaine

Durante nuestros años en Richmond, hemos experimentado un asombroso renacimiento de un río orgulloso, empañado durante mucho tiempo por la contaminación y el abandono, reclamando su estatus como el porche delantero de Richmond, la razón misma de su existencia. Ahora, el río James es reconocido mundialmente por su recuperación. Ganó el prestigioso premio Theiss International Riverprize en 2019 como tributo tanto a su historia como a su restauración. La población de águilas calvas a lo largo del James estuvo una vez entre las más densas de América del Norte, pero prácticamente había desaparecido a mediados de la década de 1960. Hoy vuelve a estar saludable y los avistamientos de nuestra ave nacional, junto con halcones, águilas pescadoras, cormoranes, garzas, buitres, patos, gansos y todo tipo de pájaros cantores, ocurren diariamente, incluso cada hora, en Richmond. El esturión del Atlántico, que se pensaba que se había extinguido en el James y sus afluentes hace solo unos años, ha tenido una reaparición notable y septiembre trae exhibiciones asombrosas a medida que estos enormes peces prehistóricos saltan del agua debajo de Fall Line.

Una vez que decidimos recuperar el James y limpiarlo, se convirtió en el centro de la identidad de nuestra ciudad, un objeto de alegría y orgullo marcado por la representación de la bandera de la ciudad de Richmond de un heroico capitán de bateau del río James. Ahora, la mayoría de las familias de Richmond, como la nuestra, acumulan maravillosos recuerdos de por vida de sus momentos a lo largo de nuestro hermoso canal.

Esta guía actualizada de nuestro río se colocará en escritorios, estanterías y mesas de café, abiertas con frecuencia para inspirar excursiones de un día y aventuras de por vida. Predigo con confianza que muchos de los que los emprendan quedarán tan enganchados al río James como yo lo estuve hace 40 años. Y la atracción del río sobre quienes disfrutan de sus múltiples virtudes garantizará que el James siga teniendo mayordomos apasionados por su protección. ≈

▲ PICTURED ABOVE: La familia Vaszquez, los padres Benjamin y Jazmin, ambos trabajadores de la construcción, y los niños Jayden, Benlen y Ashley, fotografiados aquí en el Tyler Potterfield Memorial Bridge, también disfrutan de Belle Isle y otras áreas del río.

The Vaszquez family, parents Benjamin and Jazmin, both construction workers, and children Jayden, Benlen and Ashley, pictured here on the Tyler Potterfield Memorial Bridge, also enjoy Belle Isle and other areas of the river.

▲ PICTURED ABOVE: Este grupo de ciclistas cerca de Tredegar Beach, con prisa por llegar a almorzar en Hot Chick, se detuvo brevemente para tomar esta foto. De izquierda a derecha: Armando Delgallego, Fiore King, Camryn Delgallego, Brendan Miller y Jenna Delgallego.

This group of bikers near Tredegar Beach, in a hurry to get to lunch at Hot Chick, paused briefly for this photo. Left to right: Armando Delgallego, Fiore King, Camryn Delgallego, Brendan Miller, and Jenna Delgallego.

Una Invitación a las Familias

Chris Frelke, Director del Departamento de Parques, Recreación e Instalaciones Comunitarias de la Ciudad de Richmond, ofrece el siguiente estímulo para las familias: Los invito a usted y a su familia a tomarse un descanso de las computadoras y las tabletas y volver a conectarse con el aire libre a lo largo de nuestro río James en Richmond. Explora las rocas a lo largo del río, aprenda y habla sobre la historia del Slave Trail, haga un viaje por el río con un proveedor y ofrezca a sus hijos oportunidades para disfrutar de las actividades del río: senderismo, ciclismo, escalada, flotación, remo, historia , naturaleza, pesca, natación, etc. ¡Disfrutar del río James en Richmond es transformador! ≈

Lugares

Estos son solo algunos lugares de los muchos que puedes disfrutar de actividades a lo largo del río.

Lisa Gayle y Mike Bradley disfrutan explorando James River Park.

Lisa Gayle and Mike Bradley enjoy exploring James River Park.

Ancarrow's Landing

Ubicado en el lado suroeste del río al final de Brander Street, Ancarrow's Landing tiene un enorme estacionamiento (más de 200 autos), una rampa de concreto para lanzar botes y el comienzo del sendero Slave Trail que sigue un camino boscoso río arriba.

Aunque Ancarrow's Landing no ofrece oportunidades para caminar o nadar, es un área muy visitada para otros tipos de recreación, como caminatas, ciclismo, pesca, observación de aves, picnics y simplemente relajarse en las abundantes áreas sombreadas. Cada mes de abril, esta parte del río está llena de peces en la temporada anual de desove de sábalos, rayas y percas blancas, y los pescadores rara vez se sienten decepcionados.

Belle Isle

Se accede a Belle Isle, ideal para familias, de 54 acres desde el lado norte del río por el puente peatonal debajo del puente Belvidere (estacionamiento en Tredegar Street y estacionamiento adicional en las calles cercanas). Belle Isle tiene senderos para caminatas y ciclismo de montaña, sitios históricos, pesca, escalada en roca, picnics, baños de sol, natación y abundante flora y fauna.

▲ PICTURED ABOVE: Familias de mejores amigos, (de izquierda a derecha) Ann, Dani y Leighton Ossont, de visita desde Carolina del Sur, y Eli, Emma, Emily y Elmer Ligh, habitantes de toda la vida de Richmond, disfrutan de una tarde de verano en Belle Isle. Emily y Elmer (que dice ser la persona más joven del mundo llamada Elmer) son fisioterapeutas. Toda la familia visita el río con frecuencia y disfruta especialmente de los senderos. Más temprano en este día buscaron y encontraron fruta Paw Paw en North Bank Trail.

Best-friend families, (left to right) Ann, Dani, and Leighton Ossont, visiting from South Carolina, and Eli, Emma, Emily and Elmer Ligh, lifelong Richmonders, enjoy a late summer afternoon on Belle Isle. Emily and Elmer (who claims to be the world's youngest person named Elmer) are physical therapists. The whole family visits the river often and especially enjoys the trails. Earlier on this day they searched for and found Paw Paw fruit on the North Bank Trail.

Robious Landing Park

Robious Landing Park, ubicado en 3800 James River Road, y con un estacionamiento para 92 autos, ofrece una buena rampa para embarcaciones no motorizadas. Un popular acceso al río para practicar kayak, piragüismo, paddleboarding, remo e incluso nadar desde el muelle flotante, el sitio de 102 acres también cuenta con 3.4 millas de senderos boscosos, un muelle flotante, áreas de juegos infantiles, refugios para picnic y voleibol de playa.

Rocketts Landing Wharf

Ubicado a lo largo de Wharf Street, justo al este del centro de Richmond y justo al oeste de la comunidad residencial Rocketts Landing, este sitio tiene un muelle de concreto de 250 yardas de largo que se usa principalmente para pescar. (El muelle está demasiado alto sobre el agua para nadar o navegar en bote). Paralelo al borde de la marea del río y brinda estacionamiento inmediato para 50 automóviles, este es, con mucho, el lugar de pesca más fácil y accesible en el James urbano.

T. Tyler Potterfield Memorial Bridge

Este puente peatonal de 500 yardas, de fácil acceso desde el lado sur de Brown's Island, es una oportunidad imperdible para ver el río en todo su esplendor: sus rápidos, sus aves acuáticas y rapaces, su panorama yuxtapuesto contra los edificios de oficinas del centro, su histórico restos de puentes, etc.

El puente es lo suficientemente ancho para bicicletas y peatones, sus cercas laterales son seguras sin obstruir visualmente, su pasarela es firme y segura, y su longitud es lo suficientemente larga para un buen ejercicio y lo suficientemente corta para no ser desagradable. Verá cada parte de la vida en este puente, desde bebés en mochilas y mochilas delanteras, hasta exuberantes jóvenes y caminantes lentos de la vejez. Y en el río, solo unos metros más abajo, verá kayakistas, tubérculos, paddleboarders e incluso pescadores ocasionales. ≈

◄ PICTURED LEFT: El nativo de Nueva York, José Rodríguez, vivió en Richmond durante su adolescencia, durante la cual ni siquiera sabía que existía el río y sus comodidades. Ahora, un veterano de combate discapacitado (Irak) y que vive en Orlando, esta foto captura su primera vez de regreso a Richmond en 27 años y su primer contacto con el James.

New York native Jose Rodriguez lived in Richmond during his teenage years during which he didn't even know the river and its amenities existed. Now a disabled combat veteran (Iraq) and living in Orlando, this photo captures his first time back to Richmond in 27 years and his first taste of the James.

Natación y Vadeo

El río James urbano parece atractivo para nadadores y vadeadores en muchos lugares. Pero no es una piscina. Nadar y vadear puede ser muy agradable, pero la frase clave es LA SEGURIDAD ANTE TODO.

Tredegar Beach es el lugar más seguro para nadar. Es arenosa, poco profunda, tranquila, poblada de todas las edades y adyacente a la calle en caso de emergencia. Pero hay muchos otros lugares y Belle Isle es uno de los mejores.

Es importante ser muy consciente de las siguientes precauciones.

1. Los niños deben usar dispositivos de flotación personales en todo momento, y se recomienda que todos los usen cuando el río tenga más de cinco pies en el ancho de vía de Westham. (Busque Westham Gauge y lo encontrará).

2. El río puede aumentar rápidamente, tan rápido como un par de pies en un par de horas, debido a la lluvia al oeste de Richmond. Así que preste atención a la lluvia río arriba, desde Goochland hasta Lynchburg.

3. Use zapatos cerrados. El fondo del río tiene muchos peligros naturales, como rocas y ramas, y también peligros creados por el hombre, como barras de refuerzo, vidrios rotos y metales afilados.

Esto es peligroso; incluso el agua poco profunda puede fluir lo suficientemente rápido como para arrastrarlo río abajo.

This is dangerous; even shallow water can be flowing fast enough to sweep you downstream.

④ Tenga cuidado al atravesar rocas y cantos rodados; pueden ser resbaladizos.

⑤ NUNCA se sumerja en el agua ni salte desde lugares altos.

⑥ Cuidado con la corriente del río. En el agua hasta la cintura, incluso una corriente moderada puede arrastrarlo río abajo. Y a pesar de que el agua hasta las rodillas puede parecer transitable, una fuerte corriente puede fácilmente sacarte las piernas debajo de ti y empujarte río abajo.

⑦ Si queda atrapado en la corriente, deslícese río abajo con los pies por delante con los pies cerca de la superficie hasta que encuentre un lugar seguro para salir de la corriente. ≈

Senderos a Pie y Rueda

Hay más de 22 millas de senderos para caminar y andar en bicicleta a lo largo de la parte de Richmond del río James. Hay cuatro pautas básicas para el uso de los senderos.

1. Los ciclistas deben ser corteses y anunciarse cuando adelantan a otros.

2. Se desaconsejan los auriculares para todos los usuarios de los senderos.

3. Los perros deben ir atados.

4. No utilice los senderos cuando estén mojados o embarrados; tal uso los daña.

Las siguientes son descripciones de algunos de los senderos principales.

El ingeniero de software Daniel Schep, fotografiado aquí con Kali, de 6 años, se mudó de DC a RVA hace un par de años. A él (ellos) les encanta andar en bicicleta por todo el sistema de parques James River.

Software engineer Daniel Schep, pictured here with 6-year-old Kali, moved from DC to RVA a couple of years ago. He (they) love biking throughout the James River Park System.

Buttermilk Trail
(no accesible para sillas de ruedas)

El Buttermilk Trail de 2.5 millas corre paralelo al lado sur del río y es un verdadero desafío y se considera la más difícil de las diferentes secciones del James River Park System. Buttermilk combina descensos estrechos, sinuosos y rápidos y subidas empinadas con muchas rocas y raíces.

Puede ingresar al Buttermilk Trail en la entrada de la calle 22 al James River Park. El sendero está a su izquierda. Se sube y se cruza un pequeño riachuelo. En alrededor de 300 yardas, el sendero vuelve cuesta abajo y encontrará un pequeño sendero lateral a la derecha. Este sendero evita un fuerte descenso por delante. Gire a la derecha cuando se encuentre de nuevo con el sendero principal. Luego habrá un área rocosa seguida de un área más nueva que tiene menos obstáculos y dos puentes de madera. Un poco más adelante el sendero se bifurca. Mantente a la derecha. (La bifurcación de la izquierda va hacia Forest Hill Park.)

Después de girar a la derecha y cruzar un puente, el sendero continúa hasta el estacionamiento de Reedy Creek y luego ingresa al bosque al otro lado del estacionamiento. En un cuarto de milla el sendero continúa subiendo escaleras y una rampa para ciclistas. Esta parte del sendero pasa por tres arroyos y muchas raíces que presentan desafíos.

El sendero asciende con curvas en zigzag y cuatro puentes más, luego se bifurca en la cima de la colina. La bifurcación izquierda va al lado derecho

▲ PICTURED ABOVE: Cole Pearce (VDP) e Ines Sanchez (profesora de idiomas), fotografiados aquí en Belle Isle, adoran los senderos del sistema de parques James River: "Nunca había visto tantos animales en el centro de una ciudad".

Cole Pearce (VDP) and Ines Sanchez (language teacher), pictured here on Belle Isle, love the trails in the James River Park System: "I've never seen so many animals in the center of a city."

del Puente Boulevard. La bifurcación derecha pasa por debajo del puente para llegar a su lado izquierdo. (Puede cruzar el puente para llegar a Pump House Drive, Pump House Park y el comienzo del sendero North Bank Trail).

North Bank Trail
(no accesible para sillas de ruedas)

El North Bank Trail de 2.5 millas "es un sendero avanzado que es técnico, rocoso y accidentado en algunas partes. Singletrack rápido y fluido con algunas subidas empinadas y descensos rápidos: los usuarios deben tener cuidado con los ciclistas de montaña y los peatones que se aproximan. Este sendero ofrece excelentes vistas panorámicas del río James que no están disponibles en otras secciones del parque."

El North Bank Trail viaja entre los estacionamientos de Belle Isle y Pump House Park. Ingrese al sendero al lado del quiosco en el estacionamiento de Pump House en Pump House Drive. El sendero continúa por debajo del puente Boulevard y cruza un arroyo y continúa a lo largo de una cerca de tela metálica, luego se une a un camino de tierra y una rampa de madera.

En la parte superior de la rampa, tome la carretera y después de tres cuadras gire a la derecha en una señal de alto. (Verá los letreros de North Bank Trail.) Luego avance una cuadra hasta el estacionamiento de North Bank Park y tome el sendero que continúa derecho haciendo una curva a la derecha después del pequeño puente de madera que cruza el arroyo.

A partir de aquí, el sendero es obvio, incluida una sección que se divide para ciclistas y excursionistas. La parte final está en un camino de tierra al pie de una colina de hierba. Luego gire a la derecha a través de un puente de acceso peatonal hasta el estacionamiento de Belle Isle.

▼ PICTURED BELOW: Este grupo de infantes de marina de EE. UU., de CT, FL, DC, TX, CA, WI, etc., estacionados en Ft. Lee, estaba usando su día de libertad para disfrutar de Belle Isle, fotografiado aquí en el gran refugio para picnic cerca de First Break Rapids. Aunque todos nacieron en los Estados Unidos, todos sus padres eran inmigrantes de otros países, incluidos Brasil, México, Perú, Ecuador y Egipto. Cuando se tomó esta foto, se estaban preparando para ir a nadar.

This group of U.S. Marines, from CT, FL, DC, TX, CA, WI, etc., stationed at Ft. Lee, was using their day of liberty to enjoy Belle Isle, pictured here at the large picnic shelter near First Break Rapids. Although all were born in the United States, all of their parents were immigrants from other countries including Brazil, Mexico, Peru, Ecuador and Egypt. As this photo was taken they were getting ready to go for a swim.

Belle Isle Trails
(el bucle principal es accesible para sillas de ruedas)

Belle Isle (accesible a través del puente peatonal debajo del puente Lee) tiene aproximadamente 3 millas de senderos, incluido el circuito principal plano, fácil y accesible de 1.2 millas. Senderos tributarios más estrechos y difíciles suben a la cima de la isla.

Historic Slave Trail
(gran parte es accesible para sillas de ruedas con asistencia)

El sendero histórico de esclavos de 2.5 millas fácil comienza en Ancarrow's Landing (al final de Brander Street) y continúa a lo largo de un sendero arbolado río arriba hasta fusionarse con Floodwall Walk y luego cruza el puente de 14th Street y hacia el centro de Richmond hasta el sitio del histórico la cárcel de Lumpkin. Hay una maravillosa señalización interpretativa a lo largo del sendero.

Pony Pasture Trails
(parcialmente accesible para sillas de ruedas)

Hay aproximadamente 3 millas de senderos en el área de Pony Pasture (7200 Riverside Drive) del James River Park System. Los senderos boscosos son en su mayoría anchos y de grava y fáciles. Esta área es una de las secciones más utilizadas del Sistema de Parques del Río James. Senderos de humedales (el circuito principal es accesible para sillas de ruedas)

Wetlands Trails

Wetlands (al final de Landria Drive) tiene 2.5 millas de senderos que van desde tierra estrecha hasta grava ancha, todo a través de llanuras boscosas. Esta área es adyacente al área de Pony Pasture y los senderos se conectan. ≈

▲ PICTURED ABOVE: El gerente del parque James River desde hace mucho tiempo, Ralph White (derecha) con el camarógrafo (xthevixionx) Terrell Nicholas, que es cantante (relltriplex) y ha estado viniendo al río James desde que era un niño.

Longtime James River Park Manager Ralph White (right) with videographer (xthevixionx) Terrell Nicholas who is a singer (relltriplex) and has been coming to the James River since he was a child.

Pescar

¿Dónde puede llevar a sus hijos a pescar en el río James en Richmond? Ofreceré tres puntos y métodos que suelen ser productivos.

▲ PICTURED ABOVE: Angelina Hines con su primer pez.

Angelina Hines with her first fish.

1 Camine hacia el área de Dry Rocks (al sur de Belle Isle) cuando el nivel del río esté por debajo de cinco pies y verá muchos canales pequeños y piscinas poco profundas. Seleccione una piscina que tenga al menos un pie de profundidad y que tenga agua corriendo hacia ella. Cualquier tipo de caña de pescar/carrete para niños funcionará aquí. Al final de la línea de su hijo, ate un anzuelo n.º 8, y un pie por encima del anzuelo sujete un peso de 16 onzas, y un pie por encima de eso sujete cualquier tipo de flotador o corcho. Cebe el anzuelo con un gusano o un saltamontes (o incluso un cuadrado de tocino de media pulgada). Tíralo al agua y espera a que el corcho indique un mordisco. Hay pequeños peces en esas piscinas de Dry Rocks y se garantiza que su hijo muerda y, con suerte, incluso atrape algunos.

2 Conduzca hasta el enorme muelle de concreto al que puede ingresar a través de Wharf Street, donde Nicholson Street se encuentra con East Main. Hay una gran zona de aparcamiento. Su hijo necesitará una caña y un carrete de tamaño adulto aquí. Asegúrese de que la línea sea de al menos 12 libras de prueba. Necesitará un anzuelo n.º 4, un pivote de barril (de cualquier tamaño) y una plomada para huevos de media onza. Corte un trozo de línea de 18 pulgadas y déjelo a un lado por ahora. Ahora deslice su línea principal a través de la plomada de huevo y luego ate el eslabón giratorio al final de esa línea. Ahora ate el trozo de hilo de 18 pulgadas al eslabón giratorio y luego ate el anzuelo n.º 4 al final de ese hilo. Ceba el anzuelo con un trozo de carnada carnosa del tamaño de una moneda de diez centavos: calamar

cortado, hígado de pollo, pescado cortado o incluso una bola de gusanos. Echa fuera lo más lejos que puedas, siéntate, relájate y espera. Cuando un pez muerde, la caña se contrae. Espere solo 10 minutos, luego enrolle y lance nuevamente, preferiblemente en otra dirección.

⑤ Vaya a Pump House Park y encuentre un lugar para sentarse a lo largo del canal principal. (La caña/carrete de un niño funcionará bien aquí). Ate un aparejo como el del muelle grande de concreto, pero use un anzuelo #8 y una plomada de huevo de un cuarto de onza. Y como cebo, use un gusano, un saltamontes, un grillo o incluso un trozo de tocino del tamaño de una moneda de diez centavos. Tíralo y deja que se hunda hasta el fondo y espera. En diez minutos echa en otra dirección. ¡Hay peces en el canal y eventualmente te morderán!

Para los pescadores que ya tienen algo de experiencia, hay un hecho fundamental sobre el río James de Richmond: el puente de la calle 14 se encuentra en la parte superior de Fall Line (el tramo río arriba de las mareas del océano) y es la línea divisoria de dos pesquerías totalmente diferentes. Río arriba se compone de rocas, cantos rodados, agua que se mueve rápidamente y lobina de boca chica. Río abajo tiene agua de movimiento lento y lobina negra. Upstream también ofrece bagres de cabeza plana (algunos MUY grandes), bagres de canal y varios "peces luna". Río abajo ofrece bagres de canal, bagres azules (algunos MUY grandes), tipo de pez, percas blancas, sábalos y stripers de primavera, y una pizca de otros peces capturables.

La captura de bagre de canal en ambas secciones puede tener éxito utilizando el mismo método: hígado de pollo (o algún otro cebo apestoso) en el fondo. La captura de bagre de cabeza plana grande (sección corriente arriba) es más exitosa si se usa un pez vivo (como un pez sol pequeño) como cebo. La captura de grandes felinos azules (aguas abajo) es más exitosa si se usan anguilas o sábalos vivos o cortados en el fondo. Por supuesto, el éxito para el bagre requiere probar diferentes ubicaciones y profundidades hasta que los encuentre.

Gran parte del agua aguas arriba del puente de la calle 14 es vadeable y/o escalable, y cuanto más se aleje de la costa y de otras personas, mejor. La lobina de boca chica es el pez estrella aquí, y varios métodos pueden ser exitosos, incluido simplemente llevar a la deriva un pececillo vivo a través de los lugares probables. Los señuelos favoritos para los aparejos convencionales incluyen larvas en colores tierra, señuelos para pececillos nadadores como Rapala, señuelos de superficie como Tiny Torpedo y señuelos giratorios en línea como Mepps.

Aguas abajo de la calle 14, pruebe uno de los siguientes señuelos para la lobina negra: cualquier tipo de señuelo Senko de 5 pulgadas de color oscuro que se pesque al estilo loco (anzuelo en el medio) sin peso y arroje a cualquier tipo de cobertura (costas, rocas, pilotes , tocones, etc.); un Rat-L-Trap azul/cromado de un cuarto de onza que se utiliza como "cebo de búsqueda" en todo tipo de agua; y un crankbait Bandit de la serie 200 en una especie de color gris y láncelo en cualquier lugar para sumergirse hasta dos metros y medio de profundidad.

Durante el mes de abril, American Shad, Hickory Shad y Stripers se dirigen río arriba para desovar y se detienen cuando llegan al comienzo de los rápidos del río, debajo del puente de la calle 14. Esa parte del río, la media milla más o menos río abajo desde el puente de la calle 14, se llena de peces y pescadores que pescan desde botes y desde la costa sur.

Bob Edwards con lobina negra.
Vintage Bob Edwards with largemouth bass.

Shad y stripers son los premios y las fórmulas para atraparlos son sencillas. Los mejores señuelos para sábalos son pequeñas cucharas doradas y plateadas brillantes y pequeños jigs de pelo blanco o chartreuse. Solo tíralos y enróllalos.

Los stripers golpearán una variedad de grandes señuelos de superficie que "escupen", "caminan" y "zumban". También golpearán crankbaits sin labios brillantes como un Rat-L-Trap azul/cromado y plantillas blancas con remolques de plástico rizado.

El autor con sábalo.
Vintage John Bryan with shad.

La perca blanca se encuentra entre el "elenco de apoyo" de la mezcla heterogénea de abril, y se puede atrapar en pequeños jigs de cola rizada y pequeños señuelos brillantes como cucharas y giradores en línea como Mepps. Y golpearán gusanos vivos, así como una variedad de cebos cortados. ≈

Andrew Knight con un sábalo de James River.
Andrew Knight with a James River shad.

Andrew Knight Sobre la Pesca en el Ancarrow's Landing en Abril

(Vea más de Andrew en Instagram: @rvajamesriverfishreport)

En abril, esta parte del río se llena de sábalos y stripers en desove. Use una cuchara pequeña dorada, plateada o chartreuse con una plomada para huevos de media onza unida tres pies por encima de la cuchara. Lance lo más lejos que pueda y enrolle rápido para que la cuchara no tenga la oportunidad de llegar al fondo y colgarse. Cuando lanzas, lanza UPstream; la corriente hará que su línea vuelva a bajar. Cuanto más arriba pueda posicionarse, mejor. Ten cuidado con las vides que cuelgan de las rocas; su línea se puede colgar en ellos. Tenga cuidado al agacharse para tomar la línea y use una línea más pesada, de al menos 10 libras, para que tenga menos posibilidades de romperse. Y finalmente, sé amable; en abril hay muchos pescadores y espacio limitado. ≈

Naturaleza

El río James de Richmond tiene una abundancia de vida dentro y alrededor de él. El agua más limpia y las tierras protegidas han creado una mezcla heterogénea natural de flora y fauna. Hay ciervos, castores, nutrias de río, ratas almizcleras, visones, zorros, etc. El río James de Richmond ahora tiene una de las mayores concentraciones de águilas calvas en la costa este. En la primavera, en el puente de la calle 14, el río se junta con sábalos y lubinas rayadas. Las flores silvestres florecen la mayor parte del año (el libro de David Ryan, The Falls of the James, enumera 471 especies compiladas por Newton Ancarrow), y el río está bordeado por un bosque de Blackgum, Sweetgum, Sycamore, Beech, Oaks y muchos otros. Un cachorro de oso ocasional incluso termina en el James urbano después de haber seguido el corredor del río desde su nacimiento río arriba.

La observación de aves es popular a lo largo del James urbano; más de 100 especies se ven regularmente, y muchas otras se ven de vez en cuando. Richmond es una ruta natural para las aves migratorias.

Los mamíferos son difíciles de detectar y las mejores oportunidades se presentan al amanecer. Pero puedes buscar huellas de mamíferos a lo largo del día. Los árboles, las plantas y las flores silvestres se encuentran e identifican fácilmente, y puede ser agradable identificar hojas, frutas y nueces en el otoño. Una precaución es que la hiedra venenosa abunda a lo largo del río y sus senderos boscosos. Una vez que sabes cómo se ve, es fácil de detectar.

Los remansos, canales laterales y bancos de arena del río ofrecen interesantes descubrimientos naturales: variedades de moluscos, ranas y renacuajos y pececillos, plantas acuáticas y uno de los ecosistemas más interesantes: los baches de roca. Los baches redondos en rocas y cantos rodados, a veces de unos pocos pies de profundidad, se originan cuando los guijarros quedan atrapados en una grieta o fisura. Luego, la corriente del río los hace girar una y otra vez mientras desgastan lentamente la roca y forman agujeros circulares cada vez más grandes. Esto por supuesto toma muchos, muchos años. El mini-ecosistema resultante puede incluir una variedad de vida vegetal y animal. ≈

Eventos Anuales

Aunque hay actividades y eventos diarios a lo largo del río urbano James, a continuación se incluye una pequeña muestra de los eventos que ocurren anualmente.

▲ PICTURED ABOVE: Marido y mujer Shannon Pettiford y Juan Valbuena, (de Colombia) en el Festival Que Pasa.

Husband and wife Shannon Pettiford and Juan Valbuena, (from Colombia) at the Que Pasa Festival.

Dominion Energy Riverrock
(riverrockrva.com)

Ubicado en Brown's Island y sus alrededores, este es "el principal festival de música y deportes al aire libre de la nación". Los eventos para competidores locales y nacionales incluyen boulder, carreras de senderos, ciclismo de montaña, perros de aire (saltar a una piscina), kayak, surf de remo, fotografía, video, pesca y más. Riverrock incluye muchos eventos emergentes, así como oportunidades gratuitas para probar el kayak, el surf de remo, el boulder, el slackline y más. Además, hay una gran cantidad de expositores aptos para familias y oportunidades para comer y beber.

Festival Que Pasa
(quepasafestival.com)

Este evento familiar anual frente al río muestra la diversidad y la belleza de las culturas hispana y latinoamericana a través de la música, la comida, las artes visuales y escénicas y una variedad de actividades.

◄ PICTURED LEFT: Omar Moya, quien se mudó a RVA desde El Salvador, e Isabel Marshall, quien se mudó a RVA desde Williamsburg, disfrutan todas las partes del Sistema de Parques del Río James y los eventos a lo largo del río (en la foto aquí en el Festival Que Pasa), y a veces toman sus gatos, Yami y Link.

Omar Moya, who moved to RVA from El Salvador, and Isabel Marshall, who moved to RVA from Williamsburg, enjoy all parts of the James River Park System and the events along the river (pictured here at the Que Pasa Festival), and sometimes take their cats, Yami and Link.

SECCIÓN DE LENGUA ESPAÑOLA

▼ PICTURED BELOW: Naomi McCavitt (izquierda, Thicket Design) y su asistente Casey Criddle creando un mural en el RVA Street Art Festival en Haxall Canal.

Naomi McCavitt (left, Thicket Design) and her assistant Casey Criddle creating a mural at the RVA Street Art Festival at the Haxall Canal.

Richmond Folk Festival
(richmondfolkfestival.org)

El Festival Folclórico de Richmond es uno de los eventos más importantes de Virginia y atrae a visitantes de todo el país a la histórica ribera del centro de Richmond. El Festival es un evento gratuito de tres días y presenta grupos de actuación que representan una diversa gama de tradiciones culturales en siete escenarios.

Accesibilidad en Silla de Ruedas

Muchos de los caminos, senderos y lugares del río James en Richmond son aptos para sillas de ruedas. Y gracias a la financiación pública y privada, así como a la promoción y las energías de los voluntarios, la accesibilidad para sillas de ruedas sigue aumentando. Lo más notable es la rampa de acceso universal en la sección Huguenot Flatwater del río, un área del río tranquila y libre de rápidos. La nueva rampa facilita que cualquier persona entre y salga del río.

La sección más grande de James River Park, Belle Isle, es un maravilloso ejemplo de accesibilidad. Se puede llegar desde cualquiera de las costas por puente, y el bucle principal de la isla no tiene barreras e incluye tres rampas de concreto que bajan al agua.

Del mismo modo, Canal Walk es otro lugar accesible e incluye no solo señalización y artefactos históricos, sino también obras de arte y estatuas.

Brown's Island, a la que se accede por tres puentes, es un sitio bienvenido por todos para una gran cantidad de festivales, actuaciones y eventos de todo tipo. Y el lado sur de la isla brinda acceso a quizás las vistas más atractivas del río: el puente conmemorativo T. Tyler Potterfield, que atraviesa todo el río sobre hermosos rápidos a flote con kayaks y tubos. ≈

Actividades Infantiles

Hay cientos de actividades y lugares que los niños pueden disfrutar a lo largo del río James de Richmond. El T-Pott Bridge es visualmente atractivo para todas las categorías de niños: niños en mochilas y cochecitos delanteros y traseros, así como niños a pie y en ruedas. El puente ofrece una caminata fácil, así como una carrera emocionante, y su sistema de barandas brinda seguridad total sin obstruir la vista.

Un área de fácil acceso para jugar en la arena y las aguas poco profundas es Tredegar Beach. The Wetlands es un gran lugar para una caminata sin aglomeraciones y de fácil estacionamiento a lo largo de senderos boscosos. Para los amantes de la naturaleza y los amantes de la roca, no hay nada mejor que Dry Rocks. La pesca de fácil acceso está disponible en Rocketts Landing Wharf. Los niños en bicicleta, desde niños pequeños hasta expertos, disfrutarán enormemente del Área de habilidades en Belle Isle. Y para los niños que hacen snorkel, no puedes equivocarte con Pony Pasture.

▼ PICTURED BELOW: Farmvillians Carter y Caroline Shotwell, de 5 años, en lo alto de la colina resbaladiza cubierta de hierba que da al estacionamiento de Belle Isle Footbridge y al cercano Festival Folklórico de Richmond. Carter, un consejero académico de la Universidad de Hampden Sydney, se ha perdido solo 1 de los festivales anuales.

Farmvillians Carter and 5-year-old Caroline Shotwell atop the grassy cardboard slide hill that overlooks the Belle Isle Footbridge parking lot and the nearby Richmond Folk Festival. Carter, an academic counselor at Hampden Sydney University, has missed only 1 of the annual Festivals.

Las siguientes son algunas actividades que los niños pueden disfrutar en el río.

BINGO DE LA NATURALEZA: haga una cuadrícula de bingo que enumere las cosas que se pueden encontrar a lo largo del río, como huellas de animales, esqueletos (serpientes y tortugas, mamíferos, etc.), bellotas, plumas (tamaños/colores), flores silvestres (colores), bayas (colores), nueces de nogal, hongos, etc. Advierta a los niños que no deben recogerlos, sino simplemente marcar la hoja de bingo cuando los encuentren. (Las cosas naturales a lo largo del río deben dejarse para que todos las disfruten).

BÚSQUEDA DEL BASURA: (lamentablemente, la basura existe a lo largo del río). Dele al niño una bolsa de basura (y tal vez guantes de plástico) junto con una lista de tipos específicos de basura: lata, vidrios rotos, zapatos, prendas de vestir, bolsa de plástico , tapa de botella, pieza de metal, juguete roto, hilo de pescar, etc.

DIARIO DE LA NATURALEZA: proporcione un pequeño bloc de dibujo y lápices de colores para el niño y anímelo a dibujar cosas de interés: una hoja bonita, enredaderas en el tronco de un árbol, rocas en el río, etc.

MANDALA DE HOJAS: en otoño, cuando las hojas se transforman en hermosos colores, los niños pueden colocarlas en el suelo en patrones coloridos: círculos concéntricos, arcoíris, etc.

BARCOS DE MADERA: los niños pueden recoger palos o trozos de corteza y hacerlos flotar como barcos. Donde hay algo de corriente pueden hacer carreras.

CUBO Y PALA: no puede equivocarse al ir a un área arenosa y darle a un niño un cubo y una pala de playa de plástico. Entonces puedes sentarte y relajarte. ≈

El Aviso

Si tiene la intención de continuar o entrar en el río, primero mira el nivel del río en Westham Gauge. (Google "James River Westham Gauge"). Si el nivel está por encima de los 5 pies, se recomienda encarecidamente que use un dispositivo de flotación personal aprobado por la Guardia Costera, y por encima de los 9 pies no debe ir al río a menos que sea un experto. El río se vuelve cada vez más peligroso a medida que sube por encima de los 5 pies.

Si encuentra un "problema" en James River Park que amerita atención, llame a la oficina del James River Park System (804) 646-6443 y/o envíe un formulario de "Informar un problema" que se puede encontrar en el sitio web jamesriverpark.org . Si necesita atención policial inmediata, llame al 911. Si necesita atención policial que no sea de emergencia, llame al (804) 646-5100. ≈

Kevin Dougherty (blue shirt and first aid kit) of Virginia Outside and mountain biking camp participants Trinity, Graham, Carson, Luke, Hank, Eddie, James, Ryan, Owen, Ethan, Jude, and Sean, taking a break at the Reedy Creek entrance to James River Park. Kevin moved from California to RVA three years ago with the intent to stay two years. Now he plans to never leave.

Afterword
BY BILL STREET
PRESIDENT AND CEO, JAMES RIVER ASSOCIATION

(Since becoming head of the JRA in 2005, Bill has seen remarkable evidence of the river's increasing vitality, confirmed by the abundance of nesting Eagles, full-body leaps of Atlantic Sturgeon, and the river's selection for the Thiess International Riverprize.)

The James River offers an incredible array of activities and points of interest to the Richmond community as captured and described in John Bryan's wonderful guide. Thankfully, the James River is once again a centerpiece of the community and a place to gather, rather than a dividing line to be avoided as it had been in its polluted past. Together, we have made great progress improving the health of the James so it can be a source of recreation, reflection, revitalization and renewal. However, to ensure that the river continues to be available for all of these critical human needs, as well as to assure its health for future generations, we must remain vigilant and committed to its stewardship.

Everyone living in the Richmond region has a stake in the river's health, indeed each of our bodies is 60% water which comes from the James and its tributaries. Therefore, we all must do our part to nurture this spectacular life-giving and life-enriching water source. Whether we are aware or not, all of us living within the James River watershed benefit from the James and also have an impact on the health of the river, but we can all be part of the solution as well. The ways that an individual can help the James are as numerous as the activities that can be done along the James. Please visit the James River Association's website, TheJamesRiver.org, to find up-to-date information about the health of the James and how you can help it.

I hope you have many years of exciting adventures and relaxing respites on the James River, and thank you for doing your part to safeguard its future. ≈

About the Author

John Bryan has enjoyed urban rivers everywhere he's lived and worked: Nashville's Cumberland, Atlanta's Chattahoochee, Washington D.C.'s Potomac, and New York City's Hudson. His writings have been featured in publications such as *Sports Illustrated, Delta SKY, Arts Link* and many others. His books have addressed subjects ranging from fly-fishing to religion to art to Down Syndrome and have included Introductions and Forewords written by notables such as Executive Editor of *The New York Times* Howell Raines and President Jimmy Carter. A native of Nashville, John moved to Richmond in 1981 where he headed fundraising for VCU's School of the Arts for over 20 years and later founded and headed CultureWorks, the region's arts and culture advocacy organization.

Self-portrait of the author, completed long ago.

In 1997 John published the urban James' first guidebook — the 326-page *THE JAMES RIVER IN RICHMOND — YOUR GUIDE TO ENJOYING AMERICA'S BEST URBAN WATERWAY,* for which he received the James River Association's inaugural Guardian of the River Award. More than 4,000 copies were donated for educational and programmatical purposes to libraries and nonprofit organizations throughout the Richmond region.

▲ PICTURED ABOVE: The author's largest James River bass: his 22-foot billboard, one of 15 artworks selected by jurists Howardina Pindell and Melissa Feldman for the city's 1986 Rush Hour Art Show.

John is married to artist JC Gilmore-Bryan. Their son Thomas works for Amazon, daughter Kelly is a nurse, son-in-law Justen is a respiratory therapist, and granddaughter Angelina is an elementary school student. ≈

Ally Johnson and 3-year-old Skylar Rose Hutchinson walk the trail from Texas Beach after an unexpected rainburst.

Originally from Pennsylvania and then Illinois, Steve (former microbiology professional and now a stay-at-home dad), Megan (clinical psychologist at McGuire VA Medical Center), and four-year-old Milo Enders experience the T-Pott Bridge.

(Left to right) Charlie Martin (VCU Political Science major from Alexandria), Jackson West (CNU Sociology major from Lexington), Ava Poelns (VCU Mass Communications major from AZ) and Brendan Lutz (VCU Environmental Studies major from NC).

West Virginia native Howard Morris and Siberia native Tatyana Lipanovich meditating to the rhythms of the river's flow.

Orders, Discounts, & Contact Information

CONTACT

The author welcomes communication. Contact him at **jbryanfish@aol.com** and/or Bryan Bunch LLC, P.O. Box 27471, Richmond, VA 23261.

BOOK ORDERS

Visit the book's website **(www.jamesriverlovers.com)** to order books and learn about a variety of discounts (for persons whose captioned photos are in the book, persons who provided content for the book, multi-book orders, pre-publication orders, special occasion orders, corporate and nonprofit orders, and more).

OR, simply send a check for $26.50 per book for Virginia residents, or $25.00 per book for other states (includes $19.95 retail price, shipping, and taxes for Virginia residents), payable to Bryan Bunch LLC, to: Bryan Bunch LLC., P.O. Box 27471, Richmond, VA 23261.

DISCOUNT IDEAS

- Get your employer to order corporate discount copies as gifts for employees.

- Ditto with your book club, recreation association, school, exercise group, church class, etc.

- If you're in the book, order discount copies, autograph your page, and give copies to friends.

- DEEP discount copies are available for your favorite nonprofit organizations.

- Contact the author to suggest other ideas for discounts.

The author is available for signings and speaking engagements for all types of audiences. He donates 100% of net sales to his local and national philanthropic involvements.